Group Activities for Adults at Risk for Chemical Dependence:

A Guide for Counselors, Therapists, and Other Professionals

Martin Fleming

JOHNSON INSTITUTE ®

Group Activities for Adults at Risk for Chemical Dependence: A Guide for Counselors, Therapists, and Other Professionals
Martin Fleming

Johnson Institute-QVS, Inc.
7205 Ohms Lane
Minneapolis, MN 55439-2159
612-831-1630 or 800-231-5165

Library of Congress Cataloging-in-Publication Data
Fleming, Martin
    Group activities for adults at risk for chemical dependence: a guide for counselors,
 therapists and other professionals / Martin Fleming.
        p. cm.
        Includes bibliographical references.
        ISBN 1-56246-099-4 (pbk.)
        1. Alcoholics—Rehabilitation. 2. Alcoholics—Counseling of. 3. Narcotic addicts—
Rehabilitation. 4. Narcotic addicts—Counseling of. 5. Group relations training. I. Title.
HV5276.F627   1995   94-41744
362.29'286—dc20   CIP

Cover and text design: TypeCetera
Printed in the United States of America
99 98 97 96 95 / 5 4 3 2 1

Dedication

To my grandmother, Mildred, who died during
the writing of this book. She had a great influence on me,
and she truly earned the stars in her crown.

Table of Contents

Introduction

The title of this guide, *Group Activities for Adults at Risk for Chemical Dependence,* draws attention to a specific group of people—adults at risk. Who are these "at-risk" adults? Everyone who uses alcohol or other drugs? Everyone who abuses alcohol or other drugs? Everyone who is addicted to alcohol or other drugs?

When it comes to alcohol and other drugs, there is a continuum of use. Many adults (20-25% of the population) choose not to use alcohol or other drugs at all. Some of these people may not like the taste of alcohol. Some don't like what alcohol or other drug use does to them or how it makes them feel. Still others choose not to use for health, social, or religious reasons. These people simply do not drink alcohol or use other drugs.

Other adults (25-30% of the population) choose to use alcohol or other drugs and do so with no real consequences. These people may have a beer after work, a cocktail before dinner, or a glass of wine with dinner. They have learned to control the degree of the mood swing and the consequences alcohol or other drug use causes by limiting their intake.

Some adults who use alcohol or other drugs (10-13% of the population) experience negative consequences that lead to personal, social, work-related, physical, and psychological problems. These people have lost choice over whether or not to use. They can no longer choose to control their use. They are addicted to alcohol or other drugs. These people are chemically dependent.

Another group of adults (25-30% of the population) use alcohol or other drugs in a way that results in their experiencing negative consequences such as hangovers, missing work/being late for work, financial difficulties, or DWI (DUI) arrests. Gradually, these people begin to lose control of their alcohol or other drug use and become unable to predict the outcome once they begin to use. Often, they engage in behavior that violates their value systems and causes them emotional pain. At the same time, these people begin to rationalize away the emotional pain, pretending that everything is all right. This loss of insight becomes a growing delusion that can render them unable to identify and resolve negative feelings about self, which, in turn, can result in a growing, chronic, emotional delusion. These people are the adults who are at risk for chemical dependence.

"To use or not to use?," in other words, is not the only question and not the only choice. Choosing how to use is also of critical importance. And there's the rub. Adults at risk for chemical dependence are those whose choices regarding alcohol or other drug use lead them into problems. Too often, their choices are based on inaccurate information, impaired personal awareness and lack of insight, and irresponsible behavior, or are triggered by emotional crises (death, divorce, etc.) These people often find themselves using alcohol or other drugs in ways—and experiencing consequences—that are unhealthy, damaging to relationships, dangerous, and even life-threatening.

The activities in this guide are directed primarily at the 25-30% of adults who have chosen to use alcohol or other drugs but whose use results in negative consequences. At the same time, however, the activities also speak to the needs of those adults who are chemically dependent, particularly the need to break through denial, which can lead them to seek out the more intensely therapeutic process of a primary chemical dependence treatment program.

How To Use This Guide

Purpose

This guide has been designed to help you become a more effective group facilitator. However, this guide is not a training manual. It does not attempt to teach you how to facilitate groups. Rather, it presumes that you already possess group facilitating skills and that you are someone charged with facilitating groups of adults at risk for chemical dependence— most likely on an outpatient basis—and with making referrals to primary treatment

should a group member require more help than can be given in the group setting.* Based on those assumptions, this guide recognizes that yours is a three-fold task:

1. To help group members recognize the problems they may be having with alcohol or other drugs.

2. To encourage group members to investigate personal issues that underlie their use of alcohol or other drugs.

3. To help group members draw on what they have recognized and investigated in order to make changes necessary to living healthier lives.

The overall purpose of the group activities that make up the bulk of this guide is to help you accomplish this important task.

Goals and Benefits

The activities in this guide are structured around three main goals:

- To provide clear factual information
- To raise awareness and generate insight
- To encourage behavioral change

All three goals are directed to benefit participants in the group process.

Providing factual information helps group members recognize the effects of alcohol or other drug use on their personal (physical, mental, emotional, spiritual) and social (family, friends, legal, work) lives. Accurate information about alcohol and other drugs gives group members a foundation for making good decisions that are rooted in

---

*A thorough discussion of the process of intervention is beyond the scope of this guide. See Johnson Institute's *Intervention: How to Help Someone Who Doesn't Want Help*, by Dr. Vernon Johnson.

reliable knowledge. Accurate information helps group members break through denial and formulate sound answers to questions such as:

- How do alcohol and other drugs really affect me, my family, and others close to me?
- How do alcohol and other drugs really affect my feelings—my emotions and moods?

Since facts about alcohol or other drugs alone—no matter how sound—do not necessarily affect the way people use them, the activities in this guide are also geared to raising awareness and generating insight into how their alcohol or other drug use can influence them to behave or act in ways they may not like and to experience consequences they may not like. Armed with new awareness and insights, group members are better able to make healthy choices about their alcohol or other drug use.

Behavior is the combination of knowledge, awareness, and insight in action. Putting new knowledge, awareness, and insight into action, however, requires the acquisition of new skills such as the ability to:

- communicate effectively
- process feelings
- solve problems
- make sound decisions
- resolve conflicts
- establish and follow through on goals
- resist pressure to use alcohol or other drugs by being self-aware, self-assertive, and self-affirming

The activities in this guide are geared to help group members acquire and practice such skills, which, in turn, can help them effect the changes necessary to live healthy and productive lives.

Groups That Will Profit from This Guide

The activities included in this guide foster any group process that is intended to help those who join together to deal with the problems surrounding the use/abuse of alcohol or other drugs. Such groups work to create empathy and a feeling of acceptance—an environment where critical reflection can happen without fear. Participants join to help one another understand their beliefs, feelings, motives, and goals so as to foster and gain insight into how their alcohol or other drug use affects their life-style. Through group interaction, members create new meaning and significance in life by exploring mistaken notions and then by discovering alternatives to old ways of acting, which leads them to commit to positive change (to action) regarding their future use of alcohol or other drugs.

As such, this guide and its activities are suitable for use in groups like the following:

- First Offense Groups
- Treatment Program Groups
- Employee Support Groups
- Military Level II (outpatient) Groups
- Mental Health Center Groups
- Aftercare Groups

Although the specific needs and goals of both the facilitator and the members of the above groups will differ somewhat, the activities in this guide will enable the facilitator of any such group to help its members:

- by providing encouragement
- by offering clues to behavior
- in clarifying problems and goals
- in identifying and exercising strengths
- in interpreting family/relationship patterns
- by challenging them to deal with crucial life tasks
- by helping them to integrate learning to make new choices and plans for future growth
- by helping them recognize and put aside self-defeating beliefs and behaviors
- by enabling them to take sensible risks that help translate new insights into healthy and appropriate behavior outside the group

Likewise, the activities in this guide will enable the members of any such group to:

- get in touch with feelings and learn to express them adequately and appropriately
- assume responsibility for ways they want to change
- learn to establish trust
- realize and accept responsibility for personal behavior
- support and challenge one another
- believe in themselves
- recognize new alternatives and set new goals
- learn and use problem-solving, decision-making, and conflict-resolution skills
- encourage one another to set and accomplish goals

Note: Should you be in the position of facilitating a group for adolescents, see Johnson Institute's *101 Group Activities for Teenagers,* a series of books by Martin Fleming.

Using the Activities with Groups

Sections

The activities in this guide are arranged into seven sections. Each contains activities that speak to the varying needs of a group whose members are at risk for chemical dependence. Each section, however, stands alone, and the activities included in each section may be used in any order. This arrangement allows for true flexibility in both planning and implementation.

Group Development Activities

Warm-ups

Guess Who I Am

Cool-downs

One Thing I Like About You

Tic-Tac Know

Eavesdropping

Why Am I Here?

My Secret Pal

These activities help individuals overcome their initial nervousness or discomfort so that they can become a cohesive and productive group.

Self-awareness Activities

Personality Profile

Johari Window

Life Maps

Where's the Stress in My Body?

Journaling

Stress Reduction through Relaxation

Draw Your Workplace

These activities help group members understand who they are, what they want, and what they may need to change to lead happier and healthier lives.

Alcohol and Other Drug Information Activities

Why Do People Use Alcohol or Other Drugs?

The Disease of Chemical Dependence

Signs and Symptoms of Chemical Dependence

The Use, Abuse, and Dependence Curve

Phases of Chemical Dependence

Blood-Alcohol Concentration

These activities help group members understand the effects and consequences of use, the process leading to addiction, the dynamics of the disease of chemical dependence, and how alcohol and other drugs may be affecting them.

Self-assessment Activities

Abstinence Contracts

My Relationship with Alcohol and Other Drugs

My Using History

Friendship Maps

Alcohol and Other Drugs and Feelings

Alcohol and Other Drugs and Defenses

Assessing Losses

Spin the Bottle

These activities encourage group members to take an honest look at their relationship with alcohol and other drugs and at what they need to change about that relationship.

Family Relations Activities

Family Faces

Is Chemical Dependence in My Family?

Family Collage

The Inheritance

These activities help group members recognize the emotional dynamics in their family relationships and how they can make them better.

Living Clean and Sober Activities

Visiting a Twelve-Step Meeting

The Twelve Steps

What Would Change if You Quit?

Learning How to Say No

Good Times without Alcohol or Other Drugs

Identifying Relapse Warning Signs

Helping Hand

The Grieving Process

These activities teach skills for living clean and sober, and they also introduce group members to twelve-step based community resources to which they can turn when they need additional help.

Futuring Activities

Setting Goals

What I Need to Change

Goals and Decisions

From Now On

Who I Want to Be

The Last Word

Stumbling Blocks

Group Evaluations

These activities provide motivation and tools for action that are based on the insights group members gain in the group.

Each section includes activities that furnish accurate facts, raise awareness, foster insight, and teach skills that lead to positive behavioral change.

Activities

Each activity is formatted as follows:

- Objectives
- Challenge
- Stage
- Materials
- Description
- Procedure

Objectives describe the activity's purpose and learning outcome(s).

Challenge describes the degree (Low, Moderate, High) of personal intimacy, honesty, or confrontation the activity requires of individuals.

Activities designated as Low Challenge are ideal for beginning groups, since they are nonthreatening and do not ask individuals for much self-disclosure. Moderate Challenge activities encourage group members to take risks necessary to achieve intimacy. High Challenge activities demand more of individuals and are generally best employed only once group members are comfortable with one another and have evidenced their ability to trust one another and to work together as a unit.

Note, however, that sometimes using High Challenge activities early on can be of benefit. For instance, as a facilitator, you may have only a few weeks available to work with a particular group, or a particular group may evidence a desire to get to the heart of the matter. In such cases, using a High Challenge activity early on may be appropriate. For example, "Spin the Bottle" (page 74) is a High Challenge activity that may be employed as early as a group's second session because of the intimacy it creates.

Stage indicates the group developmental stage for which the specific activity is most appropriate.

Like individuals, groups tend to develop at different rates and with different styles. Almost all the dynamics that exist among individuals also develop in a group. Thus, each activity in this guide is rated according to the normal progression of group development:

Stage 1: **Trust-building**
Stage 2: **Problem-solving/Conflict Resolution**
Stage 3: **Risk-taking/Productivity**
Stage 4: **Closure**

Although the above stages are sequential, some groups experiencing alcohol or other drug problems do not always progress through all the stages because of blocks (for example, individual groups members' defensiveness or personal dysfunction). Other groups may move back and forth among the stages. Thus, your insight into the group's development is crucial to choosing stage-appropriate activities.

Stage 1: Trust-building activities help group members become acquainted and comfortable with one another. Likewise, they also inform group members how the group will function in regard to rules, goals, and expectations. Groups in Stage 1 are concerned with issues of trust. Group members wonder:

- What's going to happen here?
- How do I fit in?
- Who are these other people and what do I want from them?
- Can I trust these people?

Stage 1 activities are designed to help group members answer these questions, gain your (the facilitator's) acceptance, and decide what they want from the group experience.

Stage 2: Problem-solving/Conflict Resolution activities help group members deal with questions of dominance and power:

- Who's in charge here?
- What's my role?

Generally, in Stage 2, group members begin challenging one another and you, the facilitator. Conflicts, testing of limits and authority, struggles to define roles are common at this phase of group development. Stage 2 activities are designed to help group members expand—and learn—new communication skills to express feelings, solve problems, and resolve conflicts in mutually respectful ways.

Stage 3: Risk-taking/Productivity activities help group members take risks and talk about what is going on in their lives. After working out issues of trust, power, and conflicts, the group in Stage 3 is generally ready to cooperate and contribute individual skills and abilities to the group task. Group members in this stage are asking:

- How can I better get what I need from the group?
- How can I best help others in the group get what they need?
- What skills must I have to make positive changes in my life-style?

Stage 3 activities help group members not only solve problems, but work together on accomplishing tasks and learning new skills that will help them live healthier lives.

Stage 4: Closure activities enable the group to come to a close by answering questions like:

- Where will I go from here?
- What should I do next?
- What are my goals for the future?

These activities, in other words, involve more than saying good-bye. Rather, they allow the group the time it needs to reflect on what has been learned and experienced and to clarify needed changes for the future.

Note: As a facilitator, when referring to the indicated Challenge and/or Stage of an activity, bear in mind that these designations are *guidelines* for choosing activities for your group. Trust yourself to adapt and modify according to the needs of your particular group. For example: a High Challenge activity might serve well to bring a new and nervous group together; a Stage 1 (Trust-building) activity might be just the thing for the members of a group in Stage 2 who find themselves enmeshed in conflict.

Note, too, that some activities are ranked as being suitable for more than one stage or even as spanning all four stages. As you choose and use these activities, therefore, remember that they are implements for teaching a concept or skill—for creating opportunities for personal growth. What is most crucial are your group members and their struggles with the effects of alcohol or other drug problems. As a facilitator, your role is to model and reinforce positive group behavior and to direct group members down the right path, assisting them to develop their own ideas and insights. These activities are tools you can use to help group members move from delusion to insight and from insight to action.

Materials simply designates the supplies you will need to have on hand to lead the group through the activity. Normally, group members should always have access to a pen or pencil and paper. A chalkboard and chalk or newsprint (or flip chart) and markers should also regularly be available in the group's meeting space. If the Materials list indicates the need for a Worksheet to complete the activity, that worksheet will immediately follow in the text, enabling you to make copies to distribute in group.

Description succinctly summarizes the focus and content of the activity, enabling you to choose accordingly, depending on the needs of your group.

Procedure provides uncomplicated but detailed directions for facilitating the activity. When specific background information is required to help you in your task, a For Your Information segment is also included.

Choosing Activities

To encourage learning and growth among the members of your group, you will want to choose activities that address the needs and goals of your particular group. Generally, adults at risk for chemical dependence need:

- Information about alcohol and other drugs and chemical dependence

- Awareness regarding their use of alcohol and other drugs

- Insight into self-worth, autonomy, and personal power

- Guidance to recognize, understand, express, and cope with their feelings (especially uncomfortable feelings that may lead them to abuse alcohol or other drugs)

- Training in problem solving and goal setting in order to remain free of the risks ensuing from alcohol or other drug use

Even given the above overall needs, however, one group may need more factual information than another. Another group's members may need help in becoming more aware of how alcohol and other drugs are the primary cause of problems in their lives. Still another group may need training in skills to help members live out their commitment to positive behavioral change.

Since you, as facilitator, know what has brought members to your group initially, you are the best judge of your particular group's needs. Thus, it is your task to determine, at least initially, group goals. For the most part, you can assume that your group members will not be familiar with one another. Thus, as a group, they are in the trust-building stage of development (Stage 1). Your initial goal, then, would be to build cohesiveness and trust within the group. Stage 1 activities would best fulfill that goal. Once group members are used to one another, you can better assess particular needs, determine goals, and choose appropriate activities to meet both.

Practical Suggestions for Facilitating Group Sessions

The following are recommendations to help you make the group experience and the use of the activities in this guide an enjoyable and worthwhile experience both for yourself and for the members of your group.

1. Once you know the number of members who will be taking part in your group, make sure that the meeting room permits a seating arrangement that allows all members to see one another as they meet. For example, you could arrange chairs in a U-shape or in a circle.

2. Since many of the activities require group members to write or draw, arrange to have tables or other work surfaces available in the meeting space. Do not place tables inside the group circle, however, as these objects interfere with group rapport.

3. Prior to each session, carefully read through the activity(ies) you've chosen to see if any advance preparation or extra materials are needed. If an activity includes a worksheet, make enough copies for all group members.

As you scrutinize the worksheet prior to the group session, take the time to complete a copy yourself and to consider what group members will learn from completing it. By doing the worksheets yourself, you learn how much time the group members will need to read and complete the material. In addition, you get an idea of the extent of information that they will get from the activity.

During the group session, be sure you complete a worksheet along with the other group members. This helps assure group members that you take the activity seriously and that you are truly part of the group.

4. If an activity requires you to make a brief presentation, style it to match your own unique method of speaking and presenting. Practice giving the presentation aloud beforehand to develop a comfort level with the information. Listen to yourself speak; practice timing and pace. Don't try to memorize the material, but do try to understand its flow so you can share its content—not its exact words—with the group. Before making a presentation, consider your own expectations. What do you want the group to get out of it? What changes would you like to see take place? Prepare yourself to share these expectations with your group members.

5. In your first group meeting, be sure to establish guidelines for group work. Consider guidelines like the following:

- Respect other's ideas and opinions.
- Focus on issues, not on people.
- Respect privacy.

If you wish, write the guidelines on a large sheet of newsprint, which you can post in the meeting room for review purposes during future sessions.

Group Development Activities

Although a variety of factors may have led individuals to be a part of your group—legal mandate, personal choice, familial concern—everyone in the group is present because they are at risk for chemical dependence. You may find that most, if not all of them are nervous and unsure of what is about to happen. Even though they all share the same problem, they may not know how to talk about it or how to work together as a team or even how a group functions. Their involvement with alcohol and other drugs has probably influenced them to "go it alone" with their feelings and struggles, and to numb and isolate themselves. Some may have developed an elaborate defense system that protects them from painful feelings and deludes them into thinking "I have no problem except the problem of being stuck in this group."

Group development activities are designed to help you break the ice, to build trust, and to encourage group members to rely on and support one another. These activities can begin to transform isolated and defensive individuals into an interdependent and productive group.

Warm-ups

OBJECTIVES: ▶ To help group members understand how group process works
To help group members talk about feelings
To energize a lethargic group

MATERIALS: ▶ Copies of the **Warm-up Questions Worksheet**.

DESCRIPTION: ▶ Warm-ups are various, brief activities used during the first few minutes of a group session to help group members talk about their feelings and understand the group process of sharing, listening, giving feedback, etc.

PROCEDURE: ▶ The first time you introduce this activity, select a question from the Warm-up questions worksheet yourself. For subsequent sessions, have different group members be responsible for the warm-up question. Group members may either make up a question or choose one from the worksheet.

This activity isn't the mainstay of a group session; it's simply a way to become focused on group process—not unlike a runner stretching before a workout. Limit Warm-ups to no more than 10 minutes per session.

NOTES: ▶ To place more responsibility on the group, ask the group member in charge of the Warm-up for the current session to assign next session's Warm-up to another group member. This process can then continue each session of group.

Warm-up Questions Worksheet

- What's an easy and a difficult emotion for you to talk about?

- Are you more like your mother or your father? Why?

- Communicate nonverbally how you are feeling.

- When somebody hurts your feelings, what do you do?

- What do you do when you are angry?

- What is one thing that you appreciate about yourself?

- If you were an animal, what type would you be? Why?

- What was your personality when you were a little child? Demonstrate it.

- What is one physical quality about you that you like?

- What is one quality that you have to offer a friend?

- When was the last time you cried? What were the tears about?

- When you really need to talk to somebody, who do you turn to?

- What is one thing that people don't understand about you?

- When you need time alone, where do you go and what do you do?

- When you think about your family, what feeling comes to mind?

Cool-downs

OBJECTIVES: ▶

To provide closure for group activities
To clarify learning
To challenge

MATERIALS: ▶

Copies of **Cool-downs Worksheet**

DESCRIPTION: ▶

Cool-downs are brief activities that bring a group session to closure and reinforce learning.

PROCEDURE: ▶

Reserve the last 5 minutes of each group session for this activity.

Choose an activity topic from the Cool-downs worksheet appropriate to the activity the group has just finished, and ask group members to respond.

When a group session hasn't been very intense, you probably won't need a closing activity. You may wish to leave it up to the group to decide or you may assign different group members to choose the Cool-down.

Cool-downs
Worksheet

■ Ask group members what they learned about themselves today.

■ Tell a joke.

■ Ask everyone to get up and stretch.

■ Hold hands and be silent for three minutes.

■ Tell the group members something you appreciate about them.

■ Ask a member of the group to summarize what happened during the group.

■ Ask group members to tell a person in group who is having an especially difficult time something they appreciate about her.

■ Ask group members what they need from the rest of the group.

■ Ask the group what they would like to do next week.

■ Ask group members if they have anything they would like to say to the rest of the group.

Tic-Tac-Know

OBJECTIVES: ▶ To increase group interaction and trust
To ease tension of new group members

MATERIALS: ▶ Paper and pencils.

DESCRIPTION: ▶ Group members gather information from every member in group and then, in turn, read it out loud.

PROCEDURE: ▶ Distribute blank sheets of paper and pencils. Ask group members to draw a framework of squares similar in style to a tic-tac-toe diagram, but with the same number of squares as there are members of group.

Once everyone has done this, ask members to mill around the room interviewing each group member in turn. Tell the person being interviewed to share something different with each interviewer that others may not know. Direct the interviewer to write the interviewee's name and the information he or she shared in one of the squares and then go on to interview someone else. When they are finished, members will have a different name and something interesting written down in each square on their papers.

Once everyone is done, bring the group back together and ask for a volunteer to be the center of attention. Have other members of the group share, in turn, what they learned about the volunteer. Continue in this fashion until everyone has been the focus of attention.

Why Am I Here?

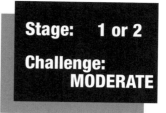

OBJECTIVES: ▶ To encourage self-disclosure and build trust
To reduce hostility and build resistance

MATERIALS: ▶ None required

DESCRIPTION: ▶ Group members explain the circumstances that have brought them to the group.

PROCEDURE: ▶ Ask group members to share in some detail why it is that they are participating in this group. If some group members are hostile and defiant, that's okay. Encourage them to be honest with their thoughts and feelings about being in the group. Encourage them to blow off some steam—after all, it's not your fault that they're in this group.

To encourage group members to be forthright, consider asking questions like the following:

- How do you feel about being here?
- What happened that got you here?
- What are the other consequences in addition to your being in this group?
- What happens if you don't attend this group?

Guess Who I Am

OBJECTIVES: ▶ To encourage honest communication
To identify judgmental self-perceptions

MATERIALS: ▶ Paper and pencils

DESCRIPTION: ▶ Group members write two brief sketches. The first concerns how they view themselves; the second concerns how they think the rest of the group views them. After guessing the correct identity of the first sketches, the group discusses the second sketches.

PROCEDURE: ▶ Tell group members that they are to write two brief sketches about themselves, one on one side of their paper, one on the opposite side. Explain that the first sketch should describe their mannerisms, how they interact with others, common moods, likes and dislikes, and so on. Then, go on to say that the second sketch should focus on how they think the rest of the support group views them. In short, what do they think other group members in the group think about them.

Once everyone has finished writing, collect the sketches and mix them up. Read the first sketch aloud to the group and ask members to guess who they think the author is. After everyone has guessed, identify the person who wrote the sketch and then read the second part—how this person thinks the rest of the group sees him or her—to the group. As you read the second sketch, pause after each specific point and ask the rest of the group for agreement or disagreement. For example, if a group member wrote, "My group thinks I am shy and quiet," ask the group: "Do all of you see Kathy as shy and quiet?"

After reading the second sketch, ask the group to make additions to it that the author didn't include, for example: "Well, Kathy didn't say anything about how she always tries to help other people in the group when they are feeling down." Follow this same procedure for every group members' set of sketches.

One Thing I Like About You

OBJECTIVES: ▶ To encourage the giving and receiving of compliments
To enable group members to take risks in a safe environment

MATERIALS: ▶ None required

DESCRIPTION: ▶ Each group member gives a compliment to one group member who is chosen to be the focus of attention. Every group member is given the opportunity to receive compliments from the rest of the group.

PROCEDURE: ▶ Discuss the importance of self-esteem with the group, pointing out that though it's sometimes embarrassing to be given compliments, it sure makes us feel good. Stress that it's important to feel good about ourselves, that we matter, that we have something to offer.

Choose one group member to be the center of attention and then ask everybody to give a compliment to this person. When all have shared something, pick someone else (or ask for a volunteer) to be the focus and repeat the sharing until everyone has had a chance to be the center of attention.

After everyone has received compliments, discuss group members' reactions to being the focus of so much good stuff. Encourage them to think about how they typically react to compliments they receive from family and friends. Ask:

- How did it feel to be given these compliments?
- Was it more difficult to give them or to receive them?
- Would it be okay to ask friends or family to give you some compliments when you are feeling down? Why or why not?
- Are you given compliments by family or friends?

NOTES: ▶ This isn't an activity for a group in its beginning stages. In fact, this activity may not work in some groups that have been meeting for a long time because of personal risk. When this activity does work, though, it's extremely effective in encouraging group members to continue giving each other sincere compliments.

Eavesdropping

OBJECTIVES: ▶ To discover new solutions to problems
To encourage feedback from the group

MATERIALS: ▶ None required

DESCRIPTION: ▶ One group member sits outside the circle within hearing range, while the remainder of the group discusses his or her problems and possible solutions.

PROCEDURE: ▶ Drawing on the above "Description," explain this activity to the group. Then ask for a volunteer. Inform the group that everyone will get a turn. Ask the volunteer to sit about five feet outside the group circle, facing away from group. Tell the volunteer to listen to the conversation within the group, but not to respond until after the group has finished and invited him or her back into the circle.

Once the volunteer is outside the circle, ask the rest of the group to discuss this person's current situation, the things about the person that they appreciate, the things that concern them, what they think the person should do to improve his or her situation.

When the group finishes, ask the volunteer to rejoin the circle, allowing him or her to respond to the group's suggestions. Discourage defensive justifications, however, reminding the volunteer that what was stated are simply opinions of other group members and that he or she is free to take what they like and leave the rest (as they say in a number of twelve-step programs).

Repeat the above procedure with other group members.

NOTES: ▶ You may wish to place the group member being discussed behind a screen. This additional anonymity encourages the other group members to share their thoughts honestly. At times you may need to steer the conversation back towards a constructive focus if group members make inappropriate comments in an attempt to be humorous.

My Secret Pal

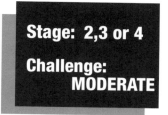

OBJECTIVES: ▶ To encourage group trust
To build self-esteem
To encourage group members to be observant of others
To evaluate growth and learning

MATERIALS: ▶ Slips of paper, hat or small box

DESCRIPTION: ▶ Group members are anonymously assigned to another member of the group. Members' task is to observe their secret pal discreetly for a number of sessions and then to give their pal his or her observations.

PROCEDURE: ▶ Write each group member's name on a separate slip of paper and place the slips in a hat or box. Ask group members to take a slip, but not to share the name on it with anyone else. Tell the group that the person named on their slip will be their "secret pal." Explain that they are to observe their secret pal during future group sessions, looking for positive changes such as risks taken or feelings being shared. They should do this discreetly, however, so that nobody knows who their secret pal is.

At some point during the last few sessions of the group experience, ask group members to reveal their secret pal's name and to share what they have observed. A group member might have noticed that his or her pal was shy at first but eventually opened up and started sharing lots of feelings, or a member might have observed that his or her pal was always helping others and putting everybody at ease.

After the sharing, process the experience by asking questions like the following:

■ What did you notice about your secret pal?
■ Did your secret pal suspect you were observing him or her?
■ How has your secret pal changed during the course of this group?

NOTES: ▶ You may wish to make the observation phase of this activity span the entire length of the group experience. The revelation of secret pal identities and the sharing of observations can be a great closing activity. Regardless of how many sessions you elect to span, it is best not to assign secret pals until the group is comfortable and familiar with each other, perhaps no earlier than the third or fourth session.

Self-Awareness Activities

Truly knowing ourselves and understanding our thoughts, feelings and attitudes is a very worthy goal. Of course, it's never easy to get a clear picture of ourselves. It takes effort and determination. It means focusing on our feelings, attitudes, and experiences and viewing them honestly. Sometimes, we'd just rather not. Sometimes we don't like what we see. And when that happens, we sometimes turn to alcohol or other drugs to drown our feelings, blur our attitudes, and mask reality.

Self-awareness activities are designed to help group members break through the haze of alcohol or other drugs and see themselves in a clearer light. In addition, by helping group members become more self-aware, these activities also enable them to recognize what they need to change about themselves in order to live a life that's really worth living.

Personality Profile

OBJECTIVES: ▶ To identify personality traits

MATERIALS: ▶ Copies of **Personality Profile Worksheet**

DESCRIPTION: ▶ Group members complete a worksheet that helps them understand the strengths and weaknesses of their personalities.

PROCEDURE: ▶ Begin this session by challenging group members to describe their personalities. Most likely they will struggle with this, as it's a difficult task for all of us.

Explain to the group that despite its difficulty, this is an important question to wrestle with. We all need to know about ourselves. Are we outgoing or reserved, happy or sad, lonely or the life of the party, quick to anger or easy-going? Give everyone a copy of the Personality Profile Worksheet to complete. Once the group members finish, spend the remaining time discussing their answers. Use questions like the following to spur discussion:

- Has your personality always been like it is now?
- If it has changed, when did it and why?
- Are you happy with your personality now?
- What would you change?
- How could you go about making that change?

Personality Profile Worksheet

Consider each set of opposite traits below and circle the number that best describes you.

mellow	1	2	3	4	5	6	nervous
popular	1	2	3	4	5	6	loner
expressive	1	2	3	4	5	6	inhibited
caring	1	2	3	4	5	6	indifferent
aggressive	1	2	3	4	5	6	compliant
patient	1	2	3	4	5	6	impatient
self-disciplined	1	2	3	4	5	6	impulsive
trustworthy	1	2	3	4	5	6	untrustworthy
happy	1	2	3	4	5	6	sad
honest	1	2	3	4	5	6	dishonest
confident	1	2	3	4	5	6	insecure
calm	1	2	3	4	5	6	angry
abstinent	1	2	3	4	5	6	heavy user
self-aware	1	2	3	4	5	6	unaware
motivated	1	2	3	4	5	6	procrastinator

Life Maps

OBJECTIVES: ▶ To provide group members opportunities to share their life histories
To familiarize leaders with group members' pasts

MATERIALS: ▶ Large sheets of newsprint and a variety of colored markers

DESCRIPTION: ▶ Group members draw a timeline of their lives that illustrates their past experiences.

PROCEDURE: ▶ Pass out sheets of newsprint and markers. Tell the group members they will have an entire group session to map out the history of their lives—from when they were born to the present. Encourage members to include anything that's significant to them: moving, parents' divorce, Dad coming home drunk and yelling at everyone, first kiss, first time they smoked marijuana, changing schools, graduating from high school, getting married, and so on. Tell participants to include how they felt (their feelings) during the events on their maps. Undoubtedly, they will want to know how to record this information, so discuss a few examples:

- **linear progression**—construct a timeline, placing significant events in chronological order;
- **boxed captions**—draw squares and sketch different scenes in each
- **journal entries**—some group members won't want to draw, so let them write out the events and their feelings.

(See the following page for a sample Life Map.)

Share the Life Maps in subsequent sessions. Ask two other members of the group to hold the group member's life map for the rest of the group to see while he or she explains the contents. Give members 10 - 20 minutes to discuss their life map with the group. If group members are hesitant to share, or if they skip over things, slow them down by asking questions. Typically, they will want to give only superficial information: "This happened, and then that happened, and then my brother . . . " This isn't what you want. Instead, ask questions which encourage the identification and the expression of feelings, for example:

- How did you feel inside when you got kicked out of school?
- What was the feeling when you found out that your daughter had discovered you passed out on the floor?

Encourage other group members to ask questions, too; this will set the stage for them to function as a group rather than to have the facilitator always asking the questions.

Sample Life Map

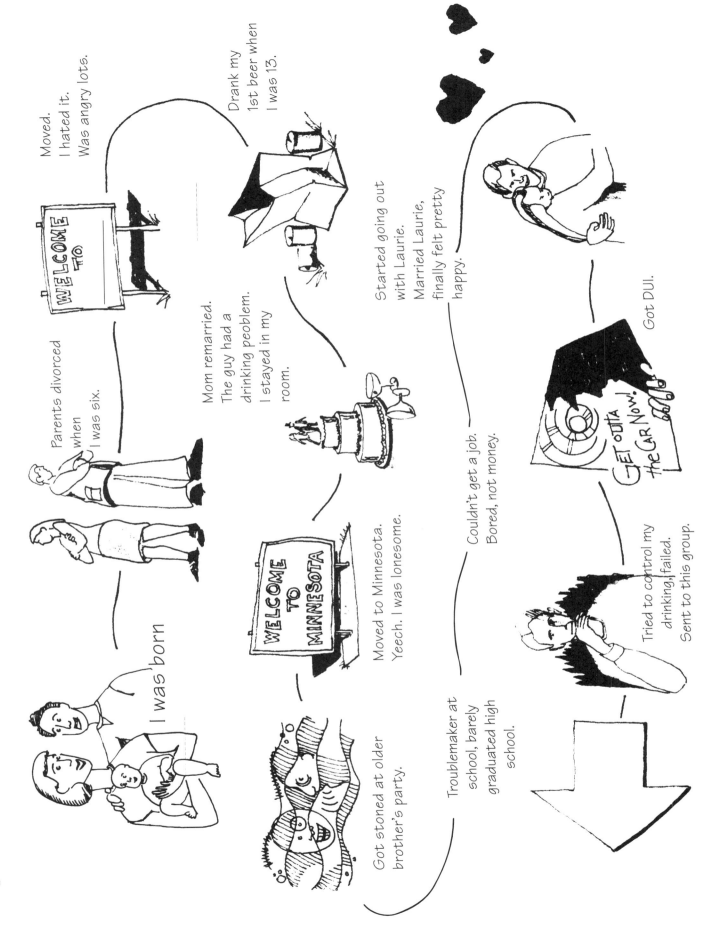

Journaling

OBJECTIVES: ▶ To encourage group members to reflect on their thoughts and feelings
To help group members recognize and talk about their feelings

MATERIALS: ▶ Spiral notebooks, pens, or pencils

DESCRIPTION: ▶ Group members learn how to record their thoughts and feelings in a journal.

PROCEDURE: ▶ Distribute spiral notebooks and pens or pencils. Then introduce the concept of journaling to the group by explaining the positive aspects of keeping a journal: it helps us understand our own thoughts and feelings; it provides an avenue for expressing thoughts and feelings that we might not ever share with others; and we can read back through previous entries and see how our feelings and problems have changed over time.

Tell the group that the first five minutes of each group session will be set aside for writing in journals. Make sure the group members understand that they can write whatever they wish, and that nobody will read their journals. They are private. Explain that they can keep their journals in the group area or if they want to write more between group sessions, they can take the journals with them and bring them back to each session. Or collect the journals after each session, assuring the group that you will keep them private.

If you wish to expand on this activity consider these options:

■ After the group has finished writing each week, ask if anybody would like to share what he or she has written.

■ Near the last session of the group, set aside one session for group members to read through their journals and then discuss what has changed during the course of the group sessions as evidenced by their journal entries.

You may either let group members take their journals home with them—bringing them back each session of group, or you may collect them at the end of each session.

Letting members take them home encourages them to write at other times during the week; however, they may forget to bring their journals to group or lose them. If you collect them, make sure you show group members that you take their privacy seriously by carefully putting their journals away in a safe place each week.

Draw Your Workplace

OBJECTIVES: ▶ To help group members communicate feelings and attitudes about their work environment

To explore the emotional relationship between work environment and personal issues

MATERIALS: ▶ Large sheets of newsprint and markers

DESCRIPTION: ▶ Group members draw personal impressions of their work location, including their office, supervisors, bosses, and peers.

PROCEDURE: ▶ Ask group members to close their eyes and imagine their office, classrooms, and other areas of the space in which they work. Ask them to concentrate on their emotional responses to their physical environment such as how it feels when they are in the cafeteria or lunch room, in a meeting, spending a few minutes talking to a superior or peer, or while working.

After they have an emotional picture of their workplace in mind, hand out large sheets of newsprint and markers and ask them to draw their place of work and the significant people with whom they interact. Point out that their drawings should focus on an "emotional picture." That is, they shouldn't try to make their drawings a true physical representation of the workplace. (See following page for an example.)

Once everyone has finished, spend the remaining time discussing the drawings. Have each member display his or her drawing. Use questions like the following to further discussion:

■ What feeling words would you use to describe your workplace?
■ What aspects of the place do you like the most? The least?
■ Are there superiors whom you could talk to if you had a problem? Who are they?
■ Has your impression of the organization changed over the time you have been here? Why or why not?
■ What can you change to make your work life a more positive experience for yourself?

My Workplace Sample

Johari Window

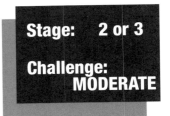

OBJECTIVES: ▶ To discover how we communicate
To learn how to communicate better

MATERIALS: ▶ Copies of the **Johari Window Worksheet**

DESCRIPTION: ▶ After hearing a brief presentation about the different levels of communication, group members identify which levels of communication they use with various people in their lives.

PROCEDURE: ▶ Distribute copies of the Johari Window Worksheet. Explain a Johari window to the group by using the following presentation.

"The Johari window is a convenient model for both understanding and explaining communication dynamics between human beings. This communication refers to much more than just language. Body language, clothing styles, sounds, and degree of eye contact also convey much of the information that is exchanged during the communication process.

"The Johari window is four-part. The first window is open. It includes information that both we and others know, such as hair color, gender, and the like. Depending on the relationship we have with the person we're communicating with, the open window will include other information: our name, what we like to do in our free time, where we live.

"The second window is called private. It contains our secrets, the things that we know about ourselves that other people don't. It includes things that we may be embarrassed about, some of our fears and dreams, and some of the feelings we might have about our chemical use.

"The third or blind window contains all the information other people know about us but which we ourselves don't know, for example, what we look like when we walk, little gestures we often use when we're speaking, or that we are very quiet. Sometimes friends and family might be concerned about our drinking or other drug use but won't tell us about their concerns. The only way we can learn about our blind window is for others to share this information with us even though the information is difficult to share and hear.

Johari Window (continued)

"The fourth window is called unknown. It contains the information about us that neither we nor anybody else knows. Unconscious thoughts and our night dreams are examples of information that are in our unknown window."

After the presentation, have group members offer examples of communication for each of the four windows to make sure they understand. Then direct group members to write several personal communication examples in "windows" 1 and 2. Point out , if necessary, why we can't complete "windows" 3 and 4. When everyone is finished, ask individuals to share their "windows." After a group member has shared "windows" 1 and 2, ask the rest of the group to offer information for the group member to record in "window" 3.

When group members are offering information to put in the third "window," make sure that they are being gentle. Sometimes group members, though not intending harm, can offer hurtful information about another group member's blind "window." Make sure that each group member has a chance to share in this process.

Johari Window
Worksheet

I Know

1 - open	2 - private
3 - blind	4 - unknown

You Know

Where's The Stress In My Body?

OBJECTIVES: ▶

To identify stressors
To become aware that the way we react to stress can lead to problems
To share ways of dealing with stress

MATERIALS: ▶

Copies of the **Body Stress Outline Worksheet**

DESCRIPTION: ▶

On body outlines, group members locate and write descriptions of how stress feels to them.

PROCEDURE: ▶

Begin a discussion about stress, focusing on how our physical bodies can react to stress. Group members may describe stress manifested in their bodies as headaches, knotted stomachs, or pain in their lower back, for example.

Pass out copies of the Body Stress Outline Worksheet and ask group members to write outside the body outline the different stressors they experience, and then to describe the different ways in which their bodies respond to stress with arrows, pictures, and words. For example, a group member might identify exams, a supervisor, her children, and starting a new job as stressors, and then on the worksheet, she might draw an arrow to her forehead and describe the headaches she gets whenever she is feeling uptight about the money troubles and arrows to her fists and describe how she always clenches her fists when she is nervous.

After everyone has finished, use the remaining time to ask group members to share positive methods they use to deal with stress. Use questions like the following to help group members share:

- How does stress feel to you?
- How can you tell when you're stressed?
- What situations are stressful for you?
- What do you do when you're stressed? Does this help?
- What else can you do to relieve your stress?
- What are common stress-related physical complaints and illnesses? Do you experience any of these?

Body Stress Outline
Worksheet

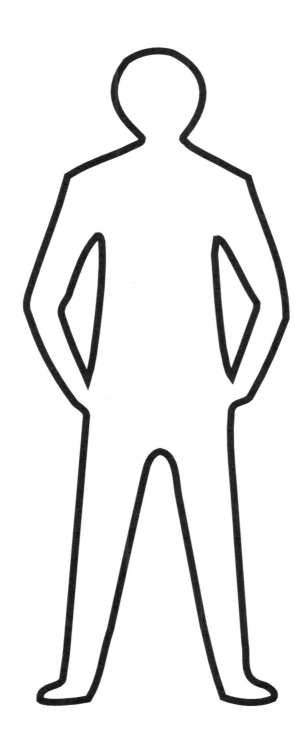

Stress Reduction Through Relaxation

OBJECTIVES: ▶ To evaluate personal stress level
To learn stress-reducing techniques

MATERIALS: ▶ Copies of the **Muscle Relaxation Worksheet**

DESCRIPTION: ▶ Group members learn and take part in a muscle relaxation exercise as a way to reduce stress in their lives.

PROCEDURE: ▶ Ask the group for examples of stress-producing situations such as exams, a new job, or family troubles. Have the group describe how stress feels and where it locates itself in their bodies, such as a tight stomach or a headache. Finally, ask them to describe what happens when stress builds up in their bodies, creating sleeplessness, ulcers, irritability.

Point out to the group that people often use alcohol and other drugs to try and relieve their stress—a couple of cocktails to calm their "nerves" or a joint to "mellow out." Point out, however, that this is only a temporary relief. Then explain to the group that you are going to teach them how to relax their bodies without using alcohol or other drugs. Point out that they can't be relaxed and stressed at the same time, so if they can learn to relax when feeling stressed, the tension will disappear.

Ask group members to find a comfortable spot on the floor to lie down, flat on their backs, arms at their sides. Remind them that the purpose of this activity isn't to fall asleep but to experience deep relaxation. Now, in a slow, steady voice, read the text of the Muscle Relaxation Worksheet.

Afterwards, bring the group back together and ask them to discuss how this activity felt.

Distribute copies of the Muscle Relaxation Worksheet to the group. Point out that they can bring about feelings of deep relaxation more and more quickly if they practice this relaxation technique at home. Once they're proficient with this technique, they can relax their bodies and get rid of stress in many stressful situations, such as before a test or a speech in front of a group, or when things are tense at home.

Finally, ask the group for suggestions as to when they could practice this activity, such as at night before falling asleep. Encourage the group to use this activity regularly.

Muscle Relaxation Worksheet

This exercise will help you relax your muscles, starting with your arm muscles and ending with the muscles in your legs. For each set of muscles, you are to tighten them for a few seconds and then let them relax. As this happens, your body will begin to feel more and more relaxed and your breathing will slow. Remember, though, the goal is to relax your body, not fall asleep. Let your mind wander and drift among peaceful thoughts and enjoy the activity. Make sure you're in a comfortable position. If you aren't, get in one now.

Close your eyes and concentrate on your breathing. Take in a deep breath until you feel your lungs expand. Then exhale. Now again, breathe in deeply . . . and then exhale. Feel your heart beat slowing and your body calming. Breathe in deep, deeper . . . and exhale. **(Pause for five seconds.)**

Now imagine an orange in your right hand. Squeeze this hand tight . . . tight . . . tighter to get every last drop of juice from the orange. Now drop the orange out of your hand and let your hand fall limp at your side. Notice the difference between the tension and the relaxation. This is how many of the muscles feel in our body when we're stressed and uptight—and often without us even realizing it. Now pick up another orange with your right hand and squeeze it, tight . . . tight . . . tighter . . . and then drop the orange and notice your hand feels even more relaxed. Now do the same with your left hand. **(Repeat with the same instruction as for the right hand.)**

Now that your hands are relaxed, let's stretch your arm and shoulder muscles by raising your arms up high behind your head. Join your hands together up behind your head and, while keeping them close to the floor, stretch them up behind your head like a cat stretching after an afternoon nap. Feel the tension in your arms and shoulders. Now hold that tight . . . tight . . . tighter . . . and then relax and bring your arms to your sides. Feel how relaxed and limp your arms now are.
(Pause a few seconds and repeat.)

Now let's focus on your neck muscles. Just like a turtle pulling its head into its shell, bring your head down into your shoulders, tight . . . tight . . . tighter . . . and now relax. **(Pause a few seconds and repeat.)**

Now let's relax some of the muscles on your face. Clench your jaw muscles by gritting your teeth together. Feel how tight your jaw muscles get when you do this. Clench them tight now . . . tight . . . tighter . . . and now relax and feel your jaw sag. **(Pause a few seconds and then repeat.)**

Muscle Relaxation
Worksheet (continued)

Our stomachs can get knotted up when we are feeling stress, so let's relax the muscles in the middle of our body. Imagine yourself about to be punched in the stomach, and so you make your stomach muscles very tight. Hold it tight . . . tight . . .tighter . . . and now relax. Take a few slow deep breaths now, breathing in deep and then exhale . . . again breath in . . . and exhale. Now tighten your stomach again . . . tight . . . tight . . . tighter . . . and now relax. Again concentrate on your breathing. You're feeling very relaxed now. Your body is heavy; your muscles loose and very relaxed. Your breathing is very slow and steady.

Now let's concentrate on your leg muscles. Starting with your right leg, tighten these muscles by stretching your leg out as far as it will go. Imagine that you are making yourself another foot taller because your leg is stretching out so far. Hold these muscles tight . . . tight . . . tighter . . . and now let them relax. **(Pause a few seconds and repeat.)**

Now let's do the same thing with your left leg. Tighten your left thigh muscle tight . . . tight . . . tighter . . . and then relax. **(Pause a few seconds and repeat.)**

Your feet also have lots of muscles that need relaxing. Clench the muscles of your right foot by imagining yourself trying to pick up a softball by stretching your toes around it. Clench your right foot muscles tight . . . tight . . . tighter . . . and now let them relax. **(Pause a few seconds and repeat.)**

Now let's finish with your left foot. Try to pick up another softball with your toes and clench these muscles tight . . . tight . . . tighter . . . and then let them relax. **(Pause a few seconds and repeat.)**

Now let's return to breathing. Feel how slow and steady your chest rises and falls. Your body feels so heavy and your muscles so loose. Pure relaxation! Take a quiet moment to enjoy this feeling. Let your mind drift and your breathing slow. **(After a few minutes tell the group to open their eyes and then slowly sit up.)**

Alcohol and Other Drug Information Activities

There is perhaps no other disease that includes as much confusion, denial, and misinformation as does chemical dependence. "This drug won't hurt you." "That drug is okay because I just use it to relax." "You can't get addicted to this stuff." People in trouble with alcohol and other drugs need correct, relevant information about the effects of alcohol and other drugs on their bodies and brains, and an understanding of the dynamics of both psychological as well as physical dependence.

But it must be relevant. They need to understand why the disease comes in people and not bottles. They need to realize what can happen when someone gets caught up in the disease of chemical dependence. And they need information to be presented in a way that is personalized to their individual situations.

The activities in this section present information to help group members begin to understand what the disease of chemical dependence is about, including the different stages one goes through. They will be challenged to explore the real reasons why people use alcohol and other drugs, and what they do to and for them. The final activity in this section focuses on the relationship between drinking, blood-alcohol content, and drinking and driving, an important topic since alcohol-related car crashes are one of the leading causes of death for this population.

Why Do People Use Alcohol and Other Drugs?

OBJECTIVES: ▶ To explore reasons for using alcohol and other drugs
To help group members identify why they use alcohol or other drugs

MATERIALS: ▶ None Required

DESCRIPTION: ▶ Group members identify different reasons why people use alcohol and other drugs and discuss their reasons for using them.

PROCEDURE: ▶ Ask group members to list examples of the different reasons that people use alcohol and other drugs, such as to sleep better, to win friends, to forget, to reduce stress. Record these ideas on the chalkboard or newsprint. When a group member offers an example, ask him or her to describe a specific situation both to dramatize and to clarify the example.

Once you have a complete list of at least twenty reasons, ask the group to look it over carefully and to decide which one of these they can personally relate to. Ask group members to share their own reasons for using alcohol and other drugs, again giving personal examples.

The Disease of
Chemical Dependence

OBJECTIVES: ▶ To help group members understand that chemical dependence is a disease

MATERIALS: ▶ Copies of the **Disease of Chemical Dependence Worksheet**

DESCRIPTION: ▶ After a brief presentation explaining the disease concept, group members break up into teams and discuss examples of chemical dependence they have witnessed.

PROCEDURE: ▶ Begin this session by asking group members why they think chemical dependence is referred to as a disease. List responses on the chalkboard or newsprint and discuss. Afterward, use the following presentation to explain to the group the major points of the disease concept.

"It used to be believed that chemical dependence was a sign of low self-control, lax morals, irresponsibility, or some other character flaw. Chemically dependent people were ordered to shape up and get it together, or they were dismissed as weak-willed or just that way.

"We know better today. We have substantial evidence that chemical dependence is a disease.

"Exactly what causes chemical dependence? The jury is still out on that question, but we do know how to tell if someone has the disease. **That person's relationship with alcohol or other drugs becomes more important than anything else in his or her life.**

"Like any other disease, chemical dependence has certain definable characteristics:

1. Chemical dependence is a compulsive and obsessive disease.
"For the chemically dependent person, using alcohol or other drugs is a compulsion. Compulsion is an irresistible urge to keep repeating the same irrational behavior without the ability to stop. Compulsive drinking or using other drugs is a primary symptom of the disease of chemical dependence. It appears to reside in the old primitive brain—technically called the hypothalamic instinctual brain—that houses our strongest instincts: to flee or fight, to eat and drink, to reproduce.

"Along with compulsion, there's also an obsession with alcohol and other drugs. Obsession means a persistent thought or desire to do something or have something, a preoccupation with it. A chemically

The Disease of
Chemical Dependence (continued)

dependent person is obsessed with such concerns as Where can I get some? How much should I get? Where should I hide my supply? Thoughts about drinking or using dominate this person's thinking and become central to his or her life.

2. Chemical dependence is a primary disease.
"A chemically dependent person has a primary relationship with alcohol or other drugs. This means that it's not just a symptom of some underlying physical, mental, or emotional disorder. Instead, it causes many such disorders. This also means that other problems a chemically dependent person may have—physical illness, disturbed family relations, depression, unresolved grief issues, and trouble on the job—can't be treated effectively until the person stops using. The chemical dependence must be treated first.

3. Chemical dependence is a progressive disease.
"Once a person enters the addiction process, the disease follows a predictable, progressive course of symptoms. Left untreated, it always gets worse.

"The normal progression goes from using alcohol and other drugs with few consequences to using them with greater and more serious consequences, including physical, mental, emotional, and spiritual deterioration. For example, a chemically dependent person might progress from experiencing a few hangovers, to getting drunk and passing out at a party or family gathering, to getting picked up repeatedly for driving while intoxicated, to losing a job, to becoming physically violent and injuring a friend or family member."

4. Chemical dependence is a chronic disease.
"Once a person is addicted to alcohol or other drugs, the symptoms of the disease become chronic. This means the person can never safely use alcohol or other drugs again. As the saying goes, the alcoholic is always "one drink away from a drunk." There's no cure for this condition. In this respect, chemical dependence is similar to diabetes, another chronic disease. In both cases, the diabetic or chemical dependent can have a healthy, happy, and productive life as long as he or she accepts the need for total abstinence.

"It used to be believed that chemical dependence was a learned behavior

The Disease of
Chemical Dependence (continued)

and could be unlearned. Not true. Even after five, ten, fifteen or more years of sobriety, alcoholics who start drinking again usually begin to drink at the same level at which they left off. It doesn't matter how much intellectual understanding they've acquired about the disease, or how firmly they've resolved to stay off alcohol. Once they take that first drink, they'll take another and another.

"Chemical dependence is a life-long, permanent disease. It never goes away. It can't be cured; it can only be arrested. That's why people who get help and quit using are often called *recovering* and not *recovered*.

5. Chemical dependence is a fatal disease.
"A chemically dependent person usually dies prematurely if he or she continues to use alcohol or other drugs. The average life span of an alcoholic is 10 to 12 years shorter than that of a nonalcoholic. In addition to the medical causes of death that are directly related to chemical dependence, alcoholics are 10 times more likely than non-alcoholics to die from fires, and are 6 to 15 times more likely to commit suicide. And drunk drivers cause over 50% of all highway fatalities.

6. Chemical dependence is a treatable disease.
"The five characteristics of chemical dependence just described—compulsive/obsessive, primary, progressive, chronic, and fatal—can be discouraging for both the addicted person and others who want to help. But there's a strong, bright light at the end of the tunnel: Chemical dependence can be treated and arrested. Seven out of ten chemically dependent persons who accept treatment and use the knowledge and tools they're given there find sobriety. People can and do quit using alcohol other drugs and get their lives back in order."*

After the presentation, break the large group up into pairs. Give each pair one copy of the worksheet to complete together. Tell partners that each is to volunteer information when possible. When the pairs finish, call the group back together and use the remaining time to share and discuss answers.

---

* Much of the information in this section, The Disease of Chemical Dependence, was adapted from the book *Choices & Consequences: What to Do When a Teenager Uses Alcohol/Drugs* by Dick Schaefer (see Resources section).

The Disease of Chemical Dependence Worksheet

Like other diseases such as cancer or diabetes, chemical dependence has recognizable and predictable characteristics. Using examples from your own life, someone in your family, or somebody you know, describe an example for each of the disease characteristics listed below.

1. Chemical dependence is a primary disease.

_____
_____
_____

2. Chemical dependence is an obsessive and compulsive disease.

_____
_____
_____

3. Chemical dependence is a progressive disease.

_____
_____
_____

4. Chemical dependence is a chronic disease.

_____
_____
_____

5. Chemical dependence is a fatal disease.

_____
_____
_____

6. Chemical dependence is a treatable disease.

_____
_____
_____

Signs and Symptoms of Chemical Dependence

OBJECTIVES: ▶

To better understand various signs and symptoms of chemical dependence
To encourage group members to look for these signs and symptoms in their own alcohol or other drug use

MATERIALS: ▶

Copies of the **Signs and Symptoms of Chemical Dependence Worksheet**

DESCRIPTION: ▶

Group members choose specific signs and symptoms of chemical dependence from a list and discuss their relevance to their own lives.

PROCEDURE: ▶

Point out to the group that, just as the common cold has a specific set of symptoms that tell us we've got one, so does chemical dependence have symptoms. Ask group members for a few examples of some of the more common symptoms of chemical dependence (for example, getting drunk regularly, getting fired from a job, entering a treatment program).

Hand out copies of the Signs and Symptoms of Chemical Dependence Worksheet. Ask for a volunteer to choose a symptom from the list, reading it out loud. Then ask another group member to say whether or not he or she has experienced this particular symptom. Once he or she has answered, have all the other group members, proceeding in turn around the circle, answer the question. The person who first answered the question then continues the discussion by picking another symptom from the list and someone else to respond to it. Continue in this fashion for the entire group session.

NOTES: ▶

When you allow group members to pick both the symptom and who will respond to it, a peculiar thing happens: Group members, aware of each others' drinking and using histories, will choose especially relevant symptoms and group members to respond. For example, Joe might choose the symptom "hangover or bad trip" and address it first to Shelly because he knows she was hung over last weekend. A certain amount of this somewhat antagonistic dynamic should be allowed, if not subtly encouraged, as it gets to the heart of the matter quickly.

Signs and Symptoms of Chemical Dependence Worksheet

1. Increase in the amount of alcohol or other drugs used.
2. Arrested for MIP (Minor in Possession) or DUI (Driving Under the Influence) offense.
3. Dramatic change in mood when drinking or using.
4. Denial of any problem.
5. Dishonesty with friends about drinking or using.
6. Failed attempts to quit or cut down on alcohol or other drugs use.
7. Association with known heavy users.
8. Frequent excuses for alcohol or other drug use.
9. Protecting supply of alcohol and other drugs.
10. Low self-image.
11. Hangovers or bad trips.
12. School or program suspension because of alcohol or other drug use.
13. Frequent mood changes.
14. Concern expressed by family.
15. Stealing money for alcohol and other drugs.
16. Using alcohol and other drugs while alone.
17. Loss of control while using or drinking.
18. Health problems.
19. Suicidal thoughts or behaviors.
20. Dropped by girlfriend, boyfriend, or spouse because of alcohol or other drug use.
21. Violent behavior when high or drunk.
22. Preoccupation with alcohol and other drugs.
23. Increase in frequency of alcohol or other drug use.
24. Increase in tolerance.
25. Memory loss.
26. Using alcohol or other drugs in the morning.
27. Loss of friends.
28. Frequent broken promises.
29. Defensive when confronted.
30. Fired from jobs.

The Use, Abuse, and Dependence Curve

OBJECTIVES: ▶ To increase awareness of difference between the levels of use, abuse, and dependence
To encourage group members to assess their own levels of use

MATERIALS: ▶ None required

DESCRIPTION: ▶ After a brief presentation concerning the differing levels of use, abuse, and dependence, group members assess their own level of chemical use.

PROCEDURE: ▶ Begin by asking group members to explain what they think the difference is between someone who does and someone who doesn't have a problem with alcohol or other drug use. They'll most likely mention obvious differences such as how much and how often a person drinks. Point out to them that there are many other indicators—why a person uses alcohol and other drugs and being unable to stop using despite harmful consequences, just to name two—and discuss some of these other signs that tell us that someone has a problem with his or her alcohol or other drug use.

Now ask the group if there are really only two categories, "no problem" and "problem." If you ask them, "Does everyone who has a problem need to go to a treatment center?" they will no doubt respond "No." Then challenge the group to break the "problem" category into separate levels. This will be more difficult for them to do and gives you a perfect opportunity to make the following presentation, which explains the concept of the levels of use, abuse, and dependence. Begin the presentation by drawing the Use, Abuse, and Dependence

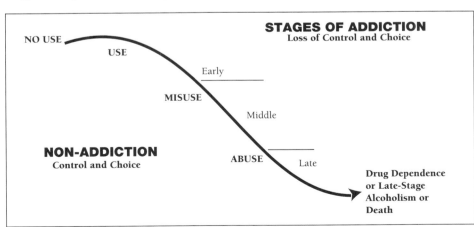

The Use, Abuse, and Dependence Curve (continued)

Curve on a chalkboard or newsprint, as illustrated here. Use this illustration to highlight the following presentation:

"Alcohol and other drug use should be seen as a continuum ranging from no use on one end of the curve to late-stage alcoholism, drug dependence, and death on the other. Although somewhat artificially imposed, it's helpful to divide this continuum into categories. Note that use through abuse is one side of the curve and dependence is on the other. This is done to illustrate the dramatic difference between abuse and dependence.

"Sometimes comparing a person who is abusing alcohol and other drugs to someone who is dependent upon them might be confusing because there can be few discernible differences. Indeed, the abuser might even appear to be using more often or even getting into more trouble than the dependent person. The real difference between the two categories lies in the fact that an abuser still has control over his or her use (whether this person wants to do something about it is a different matter). The dependent person has lost control. This is why some adults who are abusing alcohol and other drugs make changes at some point—for example, they grow up, mellow out, get married, or get a good job—while others, looking and acting just like those who abuse alcohol and other drugs, never seem to break out of the pattern of heavy use and its resultant problems. These people have crossed the line into dependence. Here are the five different levels focusing, in this case, on the drug alcohol:

No use - Many people simply don't use at all. They don't like the taste of alcoholic drinks, they don't like what it does to their bodies, or it's against their religious teachings.

Use - This category can be defined as using alcohol to enhance an already pleasurable event. Social drinking fits in this category, such as having a drink or two at a party or with dinner or special occasions.

Misuse - This category is defined by occasional problems. Someone makes a mistake and gets drunk at a wedding reception even though he or she didn't intend to. Many people learn from these types of experiences and return to the use level.

Abuse - If misuse is occasional problems, abuse is regular or more destructive problems resulting from the use of alcohol. It's characterized by getting drunk regularly. Instead of using the

The Use, Abuse, and Dependence Curve (continued)

consequences of an episode—hangover, embarrassment—as a learning experience and making changes in drinking behavior, a person who abuses alcohol continues to repeat the same mistake over and over again. The alcohol has begun to interfere in the person's life. This person still has control over his or her drinking and can make some changes and move back up into the misuse or the use level if he or she so chooses.

Dependence - Once a person becomes dependent on alcohol, he or she has lost control over his or her ability to use or not use. Alcohol is now in control. It's no different than a person with the flu saying, "I think I will be over this flu by noon today." The flu is in charge. A chemically dependent person would be drunk at the wedding reception despite any promises made not to drink this time.

We can also subdivide this category into early, middle, and late stages, demonstrating that once someone is chemically dependent, there is a downward progression towards what Alcoholics Anonymous refers to as jails, institutions, and death.

Some additional points to consider:

- Young adults can progress from use to dependence in a matter of several years.

- The longer a person remains at the abuse level, the more likely he or she will cross over into dependence.

- Making a distinction between abuse and dependence in a young adult is much more difficult because of other concurrent issues of this dynamic life stage.

- Once someone has crossed the line into dependence, he or she can't return back to responsible use. Whether recovering or not, he or she will always be chemically dependent."

After the presentation, one by one, ask group members to describe their own alcohol or other drug use in terms of the Use, Abuse, and Dependence Curve and to explain to the group at which level they believe their own use to be.

This can also be an appropriate session to use an alcohol or other drug assessment questionnaire, especially if the test results will score group members on the Use, Abuse, and Dependence curve.

Phases of
Chemical Dependence

OBJECTIVES: ▶ To discover the different phases of chemical dependence.
To recognize chemical dependence as a disease

MATERIALS: ▶ None required

DESCRIPTION: ▶ Through presentation, demonstration, and discussion, the group members investigate how chemical dependence occurs over four phases.

PROCEDURE: ▶ Begin this session by pointing out to the group that chemical dependence isn't something that happens overnight. Rather, it's a process with different phases. Explain that to better understand what chemical dependence is, it's helpful to understand what these phases are.

Ask group members to explain what they think is the progression of chemical dependence. Once the group has struggled with this briefly, make a presentation on the four phases of chemical dependence, drawing on the For Your Information section following this activity. In order to make this information more meaningful, use the group to demonstrate the four phases as you explain them. Begin by asking two group members to sit in the center of the group circle. These two group members will represent "alcohol" and "other drugs" (let them choose which one). Also choose one group member to "contract" chemical dependence. The remaining circle of group members will represent life.

As you explain the first phase (learning), ask the chemically dependent group member to enter the circle and briefly join the two group members representing "alcohol" and "other drugs." As you explain the second stage (seeking), have the group member make a return visit to the "alcohol" and "other drugs." During the explanation of the third stage (loss of choice), have the group member return to the "alcohol" and "other drugs" again, and have them grab the person tight and only let go after he or she promises to return later. Then, during the explanation of the fourth and final stage (using to feel normal), have "alcohol" and "other drugs" grab the person and refuse to let go.

After this demonstration, use the remaining time to discuss which phase group members think they may be in. As group members take turns sharing, ask them questions that require them to explain their answers in more detail, for example:

Phases of
Chemical Dependence (continued)

NOTES:

■ Why do you think that you are in this phase?
■ How long have you been in this phase?
■ Do you think that you will move into the next phase?
  Why or why not?
■ Do you know anyone who is in the third or fourth phase?

To make the demonstration more effective, you might consider taking the two group members who will be representing the alcohol and other drugs aside and explaining their roles to them privately, rather than in front of the rest of the group.

   Also be sure to mention that many people do recover from chemical dependence. Many people who were in the fourth stage are now leading happy, sober lives.

For Your Information...
The Four Phases of Chemical Dependence

Phase one: Learning: As people first use alcohol or other drugs, they learn that it changes how they are feeling, usually in a positive way. This is a pleasant experience for most people, and, once the effects wear off, they return to normal.

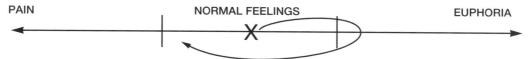

Phase two: Seeking: After several experiences with alcohol or other drugs, people move out of the learning stage and into the seeking stage. People in this stage know what alcohol or other drugs will do and knows how much they need to drink in order to get a certain effect. Unfortunately, some people in this stage use alcohol and other drugs in an attempt to get rid of uncomfortable feelings, such as anger or loneliness. This is a temporary solution, however, because the painful feelings return when the effects of the chemical have worn off.

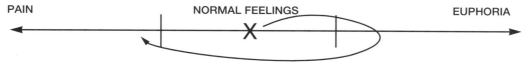

Phase three: Loss of Choice: Some people move from the second stage into the third stage. This stage signals the presence of chemical dependence. People in this stage have lost the ability to choose whether to use or not. Up until this stage, people could choose from many different ways to deal with their feelings, but now they rely on only one way—the use of alcohol and other drugs. Whenever they are feeling uncomfortable, they turn to the alcohol and other drugs for relief. So the people aren't in control; the alcohol and other drugs are.

Stage four: Using to Feel Normal: This last stage is a dangerous place characterized by deterioration in all areas of life—relationships, work, depression, physical health. People in this stage always feel bad and use alcohol and other drugs in an attempt just to feel normal once again. When people reach this stage of chemical dependence, most everyone around them recognizes that there is a problem.

Blood-Alcohol Concentration

OBJECTIVES: ▶ To discover how alcohol impairs functioning
To learn how to assess the degree of impairment before using alcohol

MATERIALS: ▶ Copies of the **Blood-Alcohol Concentration Worksheet**
Hand-held calculators, one for every two group members

DESCRIPTION: ▶ Group members learn about blood-alcohol content (BAC), estimate their own BAC and level of impairment for various amounts of ingested alcohol.

PROCEDURE: ▶ Write the phrase "Blood-Alcohol Concentration" on the chalkboard or newsprint. Tell the group that if we choose to use alcohol, understanding blood-alcohol concentration can help us discover just how alcohol affects us.

Distribute copies of the Blood-Alcohol Concentration Worksheet. Point out the opening paragraph and ask one of the group members to read it aloud. Afterward, go on to make the following presentation:

"Ethyl alcohol—the type of alcohol found in beer, wine, wine coolers, liquor, and some over-the-counter medications—acts as a general depressant on the brain and nervous system. The areas of the brain that are first affected by alcohol are memory, reasoning, reaction time, and coordination. Alcohol doesn't require digestion to begin its effects. Rather, it is absorbed immediately into the bloodstream through the walls of the stomach and the small intestine.

"The body needs about one hour to oxidize one ounce of alcohol, and nothing can speed up this process—not coffee, not exercise, not cold showers—nothing."

Divide the group into pairs. Give partners a hand-held calculator. Have them work together to complete the Blood-Alcohol Concentration Worksheet. If you wish, go through the worksheet with them, using yourself as an example.

Once partners have completed the worksheet, invite them to share results with the group. Conclude the activity by asking group members to respond to the following questions:

■ Do the numbers you found on the BAC Chart match your personal experience? That is, when you have that many drinks, do you usually "feel" the effects—for example, "mellow," "buzzed," drunk?"

■ How might knowing your blood-alcohol concentration help you limit alcohol use?

Blood-Alcohol Concentration Worksheet

Blood-alcohol concentration is expressed as a percentage of the amount of alcohol in a person's blood. Numerous factors affect this percentage, but the three most significant are:

- number of drinks* consumed
- time frame
- rate of metabolism (most closely estimated by using "ideal" body weight as a guide)

* A "drink" = a 12-oz. beer, a 4-oz. glass of wine, or one ounce of 80-proof liquor.

The BAC Chart

		100	125	150	175	200	225	250	BODY WEIGHT
	1	.03	.03	.02	.02	.01	.01	.01	
	2	.06	.05	.04	.04	.03	.03	.03	Affected
	3	.10	.08	.06	.06	.05	.04	.04	
	4	.13	.10	.09	.07	.06	.06	.05	Impaired
	5	.16	.13	.11	.09	.08	.07	.06	
	6	.19	.16	.13	.11	.10	.09	.08	
	7	.22	.18	.15	.13	.11	.10	.09	
	8	.26	.21	.17	.15	.13	.11	.10	
Number of Drinks	9	.29	.24	.20	.17	.14	.13	.12	Intoxicated
	10	.33	.26	.22	.18	.16	.14	.13	
	11	.36	.29	.24	.20	.18	.16	.14	
	12	.39	.31	.26	.22	.19	.17	.16	

Self-Assessment Activities

This section of activities represents the content of a typical group for those in trouble due to their own chemical use. Paging through this section you'll note that the activities in this section have a common theme of examining various aspects of alcohol and other drug use. Often, it's not that group members don't really know how much marijuana they're smoking or beer they're drinking—it's just that denial makes the picture cloudy. These activities help group members get in touch with reality by helping them recognize how much alcohol and other drugs they're using, how often they use, and how much trouble all of this is causing them.

You may well imagine, this isn't a pleasant process for group members who won't want to admit what they discover. Expect resistance. When the going gets rough, remind yourself that the fact group members are troubled by an activity is actually a good sign. It means that you, the activity, and the group are getting through to them. Uncomfortable as this may be (sometimes for you as well as them), it's really why they are in the group in the first place.

Abstinence Contracts

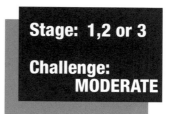
OBJECTIVES: To encourage group members to abstain from alcohol and other drugs

MATERIALS: ▶ Copies of the **Abstinence Contract Worksheet**

DESCRIPTION: ▶ Group members sign abstinence contracts containing consequences that address their specific situations and needs.

PROCEDURE: ▶ Discuss with group members the importance of their abstinence from alcohol and other drugs for the duration of the group cycle. Stress that their participation in this group is a time for them to learn about themselves, their feelings, their problems and how to solve them, and the true extent of the nature of their own use. Challenge the group to make a commitment to stay abstinent for the duration of the group cycle, stressing that this abstinence includes alcohol and all other drugs, except those prescribed by a physician.

To formalize this agreement, distribute copies of the Abstinence Contract Worksheet. Ask group members to read over the contract and fill in the appropriate blanks individually, not as a group. Once everyone has completed a contract, have them ask another group member to sign it as a witness. Then ask group members to tell the group what sort of commitment they made and whether they think this will be an easy or difficult commitment to keep.

NOTES: ▶ These contracts can help group members abstain from alcohol and other drugs, but they can also create dishonesty and secrecy in group if someone breaks the contract and is afraid to talk about it. For this reason, it's best not to put undo pressure on group members to make a pledge that they have no intention of keeping.

Of course, many, if not all, members of the group are participating because of specific consequences that brought them to the group. Thus, they are most likely already on—and should be if they aren't on—a no-use contract. This within-the-group contract should reflect their outside obligations such as going in for a diagnostic evaluation if they use again.

Abstinence Contract Worksheet

I will not use any alcohol or other drugs for the following time period:

_____ through _____.

If I break that commitment, I will take these steps:

1. _____

2. _____

3. _____

These would be my consequences:

1. _____

2. _____

3. _____

Signed _____ Date _____

Witnessed _____

My Relationship with Alcohol and Other Drugs

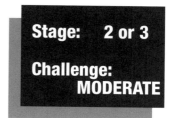

OBJECTIVES: ▶ To discover our relationship with alcohol and other drugs

MATERIALS: ▶ Large sheets of newsprint and markers

DESCRIPTION: ▶ Group members diagram their relationship with alcohol and other drugs. These drawings are then interpreted and discussed by the group.

PROCEDURE: ▶ Give group members newsprint and markers. Ask them to write their names in the center of the page and to draw a circle around it. Once done, ask them to write words around their name that describe any drugs (including alcohol) that they use and to circle each one.

Once the page is filled with these circles, ask group members to draw connecting lines radiating out from their name in the center to the various circles. In addition, ask them to signify the importance of each relationship by making the lines single, double, or triple.

After the group members have finished, spend the rest of the session discussing their drawings. Use questions like the following to spur discussion and to help members understand their relationship with alcohol and other drugs.

■ Which relationships are the most important to you?
■ Which relationships are insignificant to you?
■ Would you like to change the status of some of these relationships?
■ Which ones?
■ How would you make these changes?

My Using History

OBJECTIVES: ▶

To assess alcohol or other drug use
To become aware of the risks of such use

MATERIALS: ▶

Copies of the **Using History Worksheet**

DESCRIPTION: ▶

Group members complete a worksheet that details their experiences with mind-altering alcohol and other drugs. This information is then discussed in group.

PROCEDURE: ▶

Explain to the group that it can be informative for them to take a look at their own personal history of alcohol and other drug use—what they've used, when they started, and how often they use. Pass out copies of the Using History worksheet. Encourage group members to be specific in their answers. When completed correctly, the worksheets will not only indicate what group members have used and when they started, but will also describe how both quantity and frequency may have changed over time. This trend information is important because it will show whether their use has progressed from infrequent to regular—from experimentation to a problem.

When group members have completed the worksheets, spend the remainder of the session discussing their answers. After each group member shares, be sure to share your impressions of a group member's using history—noting variety of drugs used, amount of use, and any trends reflecting an increase in use.

Using History Worksheet

Name_____ Date_____

Instructions: This worksheet is a summary of your experiences with alcohol and other drugs—how much and how often, both past and present. Under the Past category, write in how old you were when you first used a particular drug, and then how much and how often during the first year. Under the Present category, write in how much and how often you currently use that drug. Do this for every drug you have used on the list.

(The first line is filled in as example.)	PAST			PRESENT	
	Age	Amount	Frequency	Amount	Frequency
Alcohol	13	3 beers	once a week	6 beers	twice a week
Alcohol (beer, wine, liquor)					
Marijuana (pot, hash, hash oil)					
Uppers (speed, crystal, crosstops)					
Downers (ludes, barbs, tranquilizers)					
Hallucinogens (LSD, acid, mushrooms)					
Inhalants (glue, gasoline, rush)					
Codeine (in cough syrup or in pain medication)					
Heroin (smack)					
Cocaine (snow, crack)					
PCP (angel dust)					
Other (specify)					

Friendship Maps

OBJECTIVES: To assess the relationship between our alcohol and other drug use and our friendships

MATERIALS: ▶ Copies of the **Friendship Map Worksheet** and markers or colored pencils

DESCRIPTION: ▶ Group members describe the number and type of friends with whom they associate, and discuss how these friendships affect their alcohol and other drug use.

PROCEDURE: ▶ Explain to the group members how friendships are two-way streets: their friends affect them and the decisions they make, but they also choose friends that are "of the same mind."

Hand out copies of the Friendship Map Worksheet. Have group members write their names in the center circle. Then, in the circles around it, have them write the names of the friends they've had in the past five years, including both current and former friends. Encourage the group to add more circles to their worksheets if necessary.

Once their sheets are full of names, ask group members to draw connecting lines from their own names out to those of their friends. Tell them to indicate the closeness of the friendship relationship as follows:

- triple line to indicate "very close"
- double line to indicate "close"
- single line to indicate "not so close"
- zig-zag line to indicate "former friend"

Finally, distribute colored markers or pencils and direct group members to color in the circles of any friends with whom they use alcohol or other drugs.

Ask group members the following questions to encourage discussion:

- What percentage of your friends use alcohol or other drugs?
- How does your friends' use compare to your own use?
- What part does alcohol or other drug use play in your relationships with friends?
- Has your use harmed any of your current or former friendships? How?

Friendship Map
Worksheet

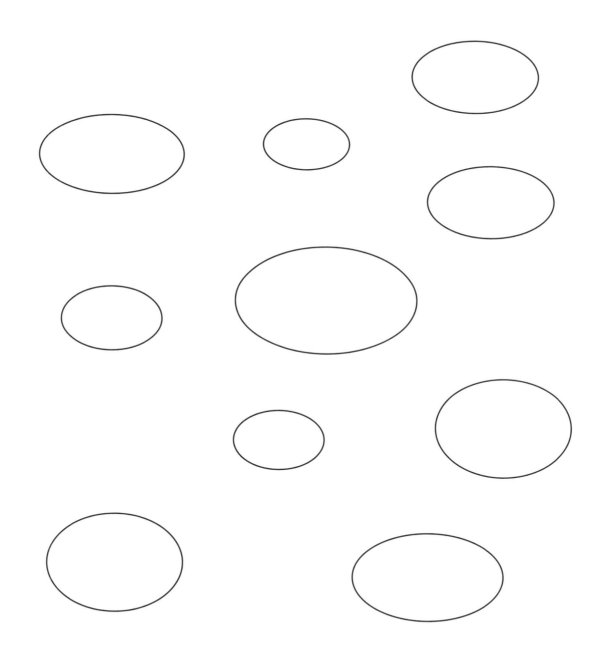

Alcohol and Other Drugs and Feelings

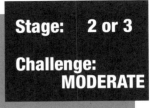

Stage: 2 or 3

Challenge:
MODERATE

OBJECTIVES: ▶ To identify the relationship between alcohol and other drug use and feelings
To encourage group members to name their feelings

MATERIALS: ▶ Copies of **Alcohol and Other Drugs and Feelings Worksheet**

DESCRIPTION: ▶ Group members complete a worksheet that focuses on feelings and their relationship to alcohol and other drug use.

PROCEDURE: ▶ To begin, ask: "Why do you think people use alcohol and other drugs?" Record the group's responses on the chalkboard or newsprint. Expect responses that include: to relax, to socialize, to have a good time, to enjoy the taste. Make sure to point out, if nobody else does, that one of the fundamental reasons people use alcohol and other drugs is to change how they are currently feeling.

Now ask the group for examples of some of the feelings that people might want to change. Again, record responses. Typical answers may include: going out drinking when feeling angry, getting high and mellowing out when feeling frustrated, getting drunk when feeling lonely. Distribute copies of the Alcohol and Other Drugs and Feelings Worksheet. Go through the directions with group members and allow them to complete it on their own. Afterward, ask them to share their answers with the rest of the group. Use the following questions to encourage discussion within the group.

■ How are your feelings changed by your alcohol and other drug use?
■ What one feeling are you most likely to want to change by using?
■ What else could you do to help you to manage this feeling besides using?

Alcohol and Other Drugs and Feelings Worksheet

People often use alcohol and other drugs to change how they are feeling. After all, nobody likes to feel angry, frustrated, lonely, or sad. Circle all the feelings that you've tried to change by using alcohol and other drugs.

afraid	frightened	hostile	lonely	sad
angry	frustrated	hurt	miserable	troubled
anxious	furious	inadequate	nervous	tense
bored	guilty	insecure	paranoid	troubled
confused	hopeless	jealous	rejected	unloved

Now, for each of the feelings that you've tried to change with alcohol and other drugs, describe an example from your own life (what drug, in what setting, what happened). If necessary, use the back of this sheet.

Feeling   **How I tried to change the feeling and what happened**

_____   _____

_____   _____

_____   _____

_____   _____

_____   _____

_____   _____

_____   _____

_____   _____

_____   _____

Alcohol and Other Drugs and Defenses

OBJECTIVES: ▶ To understand the nature of defenses
To identify our own defenses

MATERIALS: ▶ Copies of the **Alcohol and Other Drug and Defenses Worksheet**

DESCRIPTION: ▶ Group members learn the difference between healthy and unhealthy defenses and, through activity and discussion, identify which defenses they use.

PROCEDURE: ▶ Ask group members to describe what they think defenses are. Record responses on the chalkboard or newsprint. Go on to ask them if they think defenses are healthy or unhealthy. If the group struggles with this question, point out that sometimes defenses are appropriate, but that other times they can be a problem. For example, if we are upset about a personal matter, we may choose not to talk about it with our coworkers. Instead, at work we act as if everything is fine at home. This can be an appropriate defense.

On the other hand, we may blame everyone else for our own behavior. In this case we are not likely to make any positive changes in our behavior and most likely cause tension in our relationships.

After the presentation, ask group members for examples of defenses, such as minimizing, dishonesty, or anger, that people in trouble with alcohol and other drugs use. List these on the chalkboard or newsprint. If group members are unable to name a defense, encourage them to describe it and give an example. Make sure that everyone understands the four defenses listed on the Alcohol and Other Drug and Defenses Worksheet, asking the group for examples of each one. Finally, hand out the worksheet and have group members complete it on their own. When they're finished, discuss their answers.

Alcohol and Other Drugs and Defenses Worksheet

Here are some common defenses from people who use alcohol and other drugs. Below each one write three examples of a time when you have used the defenses.

Denying: refusing to accept the way things really are.

1.
2.
3.

Rationalizing: making excuses so that everything seems okay.

1.
2.
3.

Blaming: trying to make other people or places responsible.

1.
2.
3.

Minimizing: making something look less serious than it really is.

1.
2.
3.

What are some other defenses that you have used? Give an example for each defense that you list.

Defense	Example
1. _____	_____
2. _____	_____
3. _____	_____
4. _____	_____
5. _____	_____

Assessing Losses

OBJECTIVES: ▶ To assess the personal losses related to alcohol or other drug use
To connect behavior with consequences

MATERIALS: ▶ Copies of **My Own Losses Worksheet**

DESCRIPTION: ▶ Group members list the various losses they have experienced in their personal lives due to their alcohol or other drug use.

PROCEDURE: ▶ Begin this session by asking group members to give examples of famous people (actors, sports heroes, politicians) who have experienced tragedy due to their alcohol or other drug use. Usually most group members can cite an appropriate example. List on the chalkboard or newsprint. Then point out that although these may be rather infamous examples, many other people experience losses because of their alcohol or other drug use, perhaps some people right here in this group.

Hand out copies of My Own Losses Worksheet and have the group complete it. When the group members finish, spend the rest of the session discussing their answers.

My Own Losses Worksheet

Many people experience losses due to their alcohol or other drug use. Some of these are tragically obvious—car crashes, divorces, being fired—but other losses are not so clear. Consider each question listed below carefully before answering. Explain your answers instead of simply answering yes or no.

1. Have you ever lost a job because of your alcohol or other drug use? Explain.

2. Have you ever lost a boyfriend, girlfriend, or spouse because of your alcohol or other drug use? Explain.

3. Have you ever been physically or sexually abused while using alcohol and other drugs? Explain.

4. Have you ever lost a friend because of your alcohol or other drug use? Explain.

5. Are you estranged from family members because of your alcohol or other drug use? Explain.

6. List three activities you no longer do because of your alcohol or other drug use.

   1)

   2)

   3)

Spin the Bottle

OBJECTIVES: ▶ To encourage communication in group
To increase group awareness of the consequences of chemical dependence

MATERIALS: ▶ Empty soda bottle
3" x 5" index cards

DESCRIPTION: ▶ Group members play a game to learn consequences of alcohol and other drug use. Then they describe an instance when they experienced such consequences.

PROCEDURE: ▶ Prior to the session, on 3 X 5 inch index cards list the consequences of alcohol or other drug use that follow:

- hung over
- arrested for drug possession
- kicked out of school
- sent to a treatment center
- gone in for an assessment
- kicked off an athletic team
- had a "bad trip"
- attempted suicide
- gotten a reputation as a "burn-out" or "alkie"
- got sick from bad drugs
- arrested for possession of alcohol (MIP)
- arrested for driving under the influence (DUI)
- went to court because of some alcohol or other drug-related charge
- been dropped by a girlfriend or boyfriend because of partying too much
- divorced because of alcohol or other drug use
- arrested by the police for selling drugs
- became addicted to alcohol or another drug
- confronted by a relative concerned about your alcohol or other drug use
- had a blackout
- had drug-using friends rip you off
- lost a job
- dropped out of college or a technical school
- lost a good friend

Spin the Bottle (continued)

Begin the session by gathering the group in a tight circle.

Place a bottle in the center of the circle. Have a group member spin the bottle to start the game. Whomever the bottle points to must draw one of the consequence cards made prior to the session and describe to the group when he or she has experienced that consequence, and what the circumstances were. If the person hasn't experienced the consequence on the card, ask him or her to draw another card. Continue with the game, trying to ensure that each group member has a chance to draw a consequence card, but respect the right to pass. Continue playing the game for the remainder of the session.

Family Relations
Activities

No matter how long they've been adults, group members' families have had an important impact on their beliefs, feelings, and behaviors. Many people in trouble with alcohol and other drugs come from homes where a parent is chemically dependent. Chemical dependence is often called the family disease because it affects everyone in the family. In such families, honest communication is blocked, emotional and sometimes even physical needs aren't met consistently, while the dynamics of denial force everyone to play the "there's nothing wrong here" game. Statistics clearly show that children of chemically dependent parents are at a higher risk for developing the same disease.

It's important for group members to gain an understanding of what went on in their childhood and how it has impacted them.

The activities in this section will help group members understand their own family dynamics better, and they will also help them decide whether there was or is a problem with chemical dependence in their family of origin.

Family Faces

OBJECTIVES: ▶ To increase awareness of family dynamics
To assess specific relationships within group members' families

MATERIALS: ▶ Copies of **Family Faces Worksheet** and pens or pencils

DESCRIPTION: ▶ Group members draw expressive faces for, and describe the relationship with each member of their families.

PROCEDURE: ▶ Hand out pens or pencils and copies of the Family Faces Worksheet. Direct group members to draw expressive features for each blank face on the sheet. Afterward, have the group follow the instructions for the blank lines next to each face. Conclude by encouraging members to share their answers with the group. If you wish, use questions like the following to spark sharing:

■ Do the moods of your family members change often? Why is this?
■ Can you read the differing moods of your family?
■ Which family members do you feel close to?
■ Which ones are difficult for you to spend time with?

Family Faces Worksheet

FAMILY FACES

	Words that describe this person	Words that describe your feelings about this person
MOM		
	_____	_____
	_____	_____
	_____	_____
DAD		
	_____	_____
	_____	_____
	_____	_____
BROTHERS & SISTERS		
	_____	_____
	_____	_____
	_____	_____
SPOUSE		
CHILDREN	_____	_____
	_____	_____
	_____	_____
OTHER FAMILY		
	_____	_____
	_____	_____
	_____	_____
	_____	_____

Family Collage

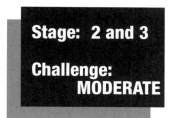
OBJECTIVES: To describe group members' families
To explore feelings related to family issues

MATERIALS: ▶ Construction paper, scissors, glue, and copies of culturally diverse magazines

DESCRIPTION: ▶ Using pictures cut from magazines, group members make a collage depicting their families and family issues .

Place a large stack of magazines in the center of the group circle. After giving everyone scissors, glue, and a sheet of construction paper, ask group members to page through the magazines and cut out pictures or words that describe their families, the problems their families experience, and the group members' reaction to their families. They can either paste on pictures and words as they find them, or first cut out all of the pictures they will use and then begin to assemble the collage.

   Once the collages are finished, use questions like the following to discuss them:

- What kind of feelings are represented in your collage?
- What are the problems in your family?
- What would you change in your family?
- Where are you in your collage?
- How have you been influenced by your family?
- How is your parenting style similar to or different from those of your parents?

Is Chemical Dependence in My Family?

Stage: 1, 2 or 3

Challenge: MODERATE

OBJECTIVES: ▶ To identify group members with chemically dependent families
To encourage honest appraisal of the problem
To help group members become more aware of their degree of risk for chemical dependence

MATERIALS: ▶ Copies of the **Characteristics of Adult Children of Alcoholics Worksheet**

DESCRIPTION: ▶ Group members look over a list that focuses on characteristics of adult children of alcoholics and discuss their reactions.

PROCEDURE: ▶ Pass out copies of the Characteristics of Adult Children of Alcoholics Worksheet . Ask group members to address each statement honestly, placing a check mark by any statement that describes themselves. After everyone has finished, ask group members to share their answers with the rest of the group, urging them to offer specific examples rather than simply "yes" or "no" answers.

NOTES: ▶ In groups for people who have experienced troubles due to their alcohol or other drug use, it's common for 50 percent of the group members to have experienced chemical dependence in their families. This session is an excellent opportunity to reinforce the high-risk nature of group members who are abusing alcohol and other drugs and who are also adult children of chemically dependent parents.

Characteristics of Adult Children of Alcoholics Worksheet

1. Adult children of alcoholics guess at what "normal" is.

2. Adult children of alcoholics have difficulty in following a project through from beginning to end.

3. Adult children of alcoholics lie when it would be just as easy to tell the truth.

4. Adult children of alcoholics judge themselves without mercy.

5. Adult children of alcoholics have difficulty having fun.

6. Adult children of alcoholics take themselves very seriously.

7. Adult children of alcoholics have difficulty with intimate relationships.

8. Adult children of alcoholics overreact to changes over which they have no control.

9. Adult children of alcoholics constantly seek approval and affirmation.

10. Adult children of alcoholics feel that they are different from other people.

11. Adult children of alcoholics are either super responsible or super irresponsible.

12. Adult children of alcoholics are extremely loyal, even in the face of evidence that the loyalty is undeserved.

13. Adult children of alcoholics are impulsive.

14. Adult children of alcoholics are at high risk for developing their own problems with alcohol or other drugs.

Adapted from Woititz, Janet Geringer. *Adult Children Of Alcoholics*. Deerfield Beach, FL: Health Communications, Inc., 1983.

The Inheritance

OBJECTIVES: ▶
To increase awareness of the genetic predisposition to chemical dependence
To encourage abstinence from alcohol and other drugs

MATERIALS: ▶
Video (optional)

DESCRIPTION: ▶
Group members are presented information concerning their genetic and environmental predisposition to chemical dependence. This information is presented through a combination of video, lecture, and discussion. Alternative activities to a video are also discussed.

PROCEDURE: ▶
Begin this activity by presenting some basic facts about genetic predisposition. Draw on the For Your Information section below.

Afterward, begin a discussion to help group members connect this information with their own families. Further this discussion with questions like the following:

■ Does your family have a history of chemical dependence?
■ Do you think you are at risk for becoming chemically dependent? Why or why not?
■ Do you think chemical dependence is passed on genetically, or is it learned through modeling parents' drinking behaviors, or does it stem from the fact that children of chemically dependent parents often have traumatic childhoods?
■ Can you identify a history of chemical dependence in your extended family?

NOTES: ▶
You can enhance this activity by using one of the Johnson Institute videos included in the Resources list at the end of this book on page 114.

For Your Information

Chemical Dependence—Learned or Inherited?

Much has been written concerning the relationship between parents' chemical dependence and their sons' or daughters' alcohol or other drug use. Everyone agrees that the children of parents who are chemically dependent are at high risk for becoming chemically dependent themselves later in life. What isn't clear is exactly how this relationship is passed on from parent to child. There are different theories.

First, some believe in genetic predisposition, that is, the idea that having a biological parent who is chemically dependent puts a person at risk for becoming chemically dependent. Research demonstrates that children of alcoholics who are adopted into healthy families as infants still show high rates of alcoholism when they grow up. In fact, geneticists claim to have been able to identify the individual gene they think is responsible for transmitting alcoholism.

Second, other people say that common sense supports the idea that, since children's primary role models are their parents, children of chemically dependent parents also become high risk simply by modeling what they see their parents doing—which is, in this case, a lot of drinking or using other drugs. Children learn a harmful lesson when they see a parent drink every time she or he is in trouble.

Third, still other people point to the fact that children of chemically dependent parents grow up in turbulent, painful, and dysfunctional home environments. Simply put, these children have a painful childhood and carry these problems around with them, eventually turning to alcohol or other drugs for escape and relief.

All of this boils down to the classic nature vs. nurture controversy for which there are few simple answers. The current opinion of the majority of professionals is that the answer is a combination of all three factors, each contributing to the amount of risk.

Here are some current statistics:
- More than half of all alcoholics have an alcoholic parent.
- Children of alcoholics are at high risk of developing alcoholism themselves or marrying someone who is or will become alcoholic.
- Forty percent of those involved in Al-Anon have an alcoholic parent, and most of this number proceeded to marry an alcoholic.
- The single most important predictor of alcoholism for a child is having an alcoholic parent.
- Fifty-eight percent of children with an alcoholic parent will become alcoholic themselves.
- Thirty percent of children with an alcoholic parent will marry an alcoholic.

Living Clean and Sober Activities

One of the fundamental goals for this group is to help some of the group members make the transition into a life-style free from alcohol and other drugs. This can be difficult to do when people's lives have been surrounded by alcohol and other drugs and the life-style accompanying their use. Even when they realize they need to quit, many group members won't know how to live without using. Group members need some tools and the wherewithal to use them. The activities in this section are designed to provide both.

You'll notice a strong emphasis on Twelve-step groups, such as Alcoholics Anonymous. This support system is free, readily available across the country, and one of the most successful of group processes. Simply put, it's a group of people who've been there and back and are ready and willing to help newcomers do the same. This is evidenced in one of A.A.'s group slogans: "We keep what we have by giving it away."

Visiting a Twelve-Step Meeting

OBJECTIVES: ▶ To become aware of community resources.
To encourage appropriate group members to begin attending Twelve-step groups.

MATERIALS: ▶ None required

DESCRIPTION: ▶ Group members visit an open Alcoholics Anonymous (A.A.) or Narcotics Anonymous (N.A.) meeting and then discuss their experiences at the following group session.

PROCEDURE: ▶ Obtain a copy of the Twelve-step meeting schedule for your community and identify which meetings are closed and which are open. Closed meetings are only for people who have a drinking problem—in the case of A.A.—while open meetings are for anyone to come and see what the group is all about. This includes family or friends of a member, journalists, or anyone interested in learning more about the particular Twelve-step group. Usually meeting schedules designate open and closed meetings (contact your local Alcoholics Anonymous clubhouse or hotline phone number for more information).

After determining which meetings are open, arrange for your group members to attend an open A.A. or N.A. meeting, either all together or less formally in several smaller groupings. The following session, ask group members to discuss their impressions and experiences.

When you meet with the group, use the questions below to help group members discuss their impressions and experiences:

■ How were you feeling when you first entered the meeting room? When the meeting was over?
■ What did the speakers have in common?
■ What was the mood in the meeting room?
■ What did you hear during the meeting that was helpful for you?
■ What did you hear during the meeting that you disagreed with?
■ How would you describe the meeting?
■ Would this group be of help to you?

NOTES: ▶ Group members usually don't like this assignment. Often this reaction stems from fear concerning a new and unknown situation.

Encouraging them to go together reduces this uneasiness. Since your group members are participating in your group because of the consequences of their alcohol or other drug use, you could make visiting a Twelve-step group a requirement for completion of the group program. Offer to take group members to a Twelve-step meeting. This will further reduce any anxiety.

The Twelve Steps

OBJECTIVES: ▶ To understand the Twelve Steps
To encourage using the Twelve Steps to help abstain from alcohol and other drugs

MATERIALS: ▶ Copies of the **Twelve Step Worksheet**

DESCRIPTION: ▶ Group members learn and then give examples of how the Twelve Steps can help people with drinking or other drug problems.

PROCEDURE: ▶ Begin this session by giving group members copies of the Twelve Steps Worksheet. Go through the sheet with the group members, encouraging them to ask any questions they may have. Then, draw attention to the questions at the end of the worksheet and have group members write out their answers. Tell them that they'll be coming back to these questions later in the session.

Explain to the group that they are going to create a fictitious person called "Jack," who is chemically dependent. To begin, have the group describe various aspects of Jack's chemical dependence problem, such as use patterns, effects on friends, work performance, family tension, and so on. Help the group along by making notes on the chalkboard.

Once Jack has been described, assign the various Twelve Steps to group members by numbering off around the group until all Twelve Steps have been assigned. Take the First Step yourself. Note: it's okay if more than one Step is assigned to a group member.

Now tell the group that they're going to help Jack get sober by helping him work the Steps. Have each group member think about how Jack would use his or her assigned step to help himself get sober. After giving them a few minutes to think about this, begin by describing how Jack could work the First Step. For example, you might say, "Jack didn't really want to admit that he had a drinking problem. Whenever anyone mentioned it to him, he got really angry and defensive. But one night, his girlfriend broke up with him because she had had enough of his being drunk all the time. That's when he realized he really did have a problem."

Then, ask the group member assigned the Second Step to continue the process. After that, call on the group member with the Third Step, and so on.

To conclude the session, ask group members to look at the answers they wrote on their worksheets. Call on them to share their responses and how the Twelve Steps would work in their lives.

The Twelve Steps*
Worksheet

1. We admitted we were powerless over alcohol—that our lives had become unmanageable.

2. Came to believe that a Power greater than ourselves could restore us to sanity.

3. Made a decision to turn our will and our lives over to the care of God as we understood Him.

4. Made a searching and fearless moral inventory of ourselves.

5. Admitted to God, to ourselves, and to another human being the exact nature of our wrongs.

6. Were entirely ready to have God remove all these defects of character.

7. Humbly asked Him to remove our shortcomings.

8. Made a list of all persons we had harmed, and became willing to make amends to them all.

9. Made direct amends to such people whenever possible, except when to do so would injure them or others.

10. Continued to take personal inventory and when we were wrong promptly admitted it.

11. Sought through prayer and meditation to improve our conscious contact with God as we understood Him, praying only for knowledge of His will for us and the power to carry that out.

12. Having had a spiritual awakening as a result of these steps, we tried to carry this message to alcoholics, and to practice these principles in all our affairs.

Write your responses to the following questions:

Why do you think it's important to list all the wrongdoings and hurts you've caused others?

_____

_____

Which step would be the most difficult for you? Why?

_____

_____

What is a higher power for you?

_____

_____

Would working these steps be helpful for you? How?

_____

_____

What Would Change If You Quit?

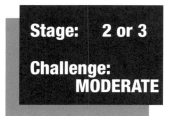

OBJECTIVES: ▶ To identify positive results of quitting using alcohol and other drugs
To encourage group members to quit using alcohol and other drugs

MATERIALS: ▶ Sheets of writing paper

DESCRIPTION: ▶ Group members examine how their lives would change if they were to quit using alcohol and other drugs.

PROCEDURE: ▶ Ask group members to list on the chalkboard or newsprint the positive things that can happen when a person quits using alcohol and other drugs. Typical examples may include success at work, fewer arguments at home, no chance of getting arrested, having more money.

Once a list has been made, distribute sheets of paper and ask group members to write at least five things that would change for them personally if they were to quit using alcohol and other drugs. Once everyone has finished, ask members to share their answers with the group and to explain why and how the change would take place. If someone is unable or unwilling to outline any positive changes that would take place if he or she were to quit, ask the rest of the group to suggest things that they think would change for the person.

Learning How to Say No

OBJECTIVES: ▶ To identify ways to resist pressure to use alcohol and other drugs
To practice using these new skills

MATERIALS: ▶ Optional: theatrical props

DESCRIPTION: ▶ Group members identify, through group discussion and with help from the group leader, techniques for resisting pressure to use alcohol or other drugs. These new skills are practiced through role-playing.

PROCEDURE: ▶ After introducing the topic, ask group members to list different methods for resisting pressure to use alcohol or other drugs. The examples can be both strategies the group members have used before or ideas they think would work. Typical examples include saying "No thanks. I don't feel like it," walking away from the person offering the beer or joint, or saying "Naw. I've got to go to work in an hour." If the group is having difficulty suggesting examples, ask them to think of a particular situation first and then think of the response. Ask them how they would handle someone offering them a joint at a party, for example. Record ideas on the chalkboard or newsprint.

From the list, have the group choose one idea to role-play. Ask for volunteers for the various parts: for example, one group member to say no, a group member to offer the beer or joint, several others to play supporting roles such as other party-goers.

Once the roles are assigned, give the group members a few minutes to create a short role-play. You might want to tell them to go over into the corner of the room, away from the rest of the group, to work out the details. When they are ready, have them present the role-play to the rest of the group.

When they finish the role-play, discuss it with the whole group. Ask:
■ Has anyone been in this type of situation before?
■ Was it difficult or easy to handle?
■ What are some other responses that could be used in this situation?
Depending on remaining time, ask the group to act out other situations from the list.

NOTES: If group members have a tough time getting into the character of their roles, help out by playing a role yourself. It can also be helpful to select group members who are natural clowns for the initial role-play. If you wish, provide props to make the role-play realistic: an empty beer can, taped party music, a steering wheel, etc.

Good Times Without Alcohol and Other Drugs

OBJECTIVES: ▶ To discover new ways of having fun without using alcohol or other drugs. To encourage group members to begin to have fun without the use of alcohol and other drugs

DESCRIPTION: ▶ Group members discuss ways to recreate without using alcohol and other drugs and make a commitment to try one new activity.

PROCEDURE: ▶ Point out to the group that many adults who have been heavily involved with alcohol and other drugs don't know any other way of having a good time than to get high or drunk. Challenge the group to make a list on the chalkboard or newsprint of all the ways they can think of to have fun that don't involve using alcohol and other drugs. When a group member offers an example, ask her to describe a time when she has participated in that form of recreation. For example, a group member might offer skiing as an example of something to do that doesn't involve alcohol and other drugs; then she should describe a time that she went skiing and the fun she had. Besides the dramatic and exciting examples that the group will typically name, ask them to also think of examples that are easy to do, have little or no cost, and are readily available, such as going bike riding with a friend, taking a walk with your spouse, seeing a good movie, playing the guitar.

Once there's a good list on the board (don't hesitate to help out if group members miss any obvious examples), ask group members to pick an example from the list they haven't experienced before that they would be willing and able to try during the next few weeks. Make sure the group understands you're asking them to make a commitment to do this activity, and that they should pick an activity that will be possible for them to try. Choose a specific future group session in which to discuss the results of their activities, so that group members know they have a deadline for completing the activity. In that follow-up session, use questions like the following to help group members describe their activities and how they felt about them:

- Was this activity enjoyable?
- What did you like about it?
- Is this something that you will do again? Why or why not?
- What's different about recreation without alcohol and other drugs as compared to recreation with them?
- What are the negative aspects of using alcohol and other drugs while recreating?
- Is it difficult to have a good time without drinking or getting high?

Identifying Relapse Warning Signs

OBJECTIVES: ▶
To plan ways to maintain sobriety
To become more aware of the signs leading to a relapse

MATERIALS: ▶
Copies of the **Relapse Warning Signs Worksheet**

DESCRIPTION: ▶
Group members identify their own relapse warning signs and construct a plan to help themselves in the event they are close to a relapse episode.

PROCEDURE: ▶
Explain to the group that relapses don't simply just happen—they have a beginning, middle, and end—and that most often there are signs leading to relapse. Tell the group that knowing and heeding these signs can help them remain sober.

List the following warning signs of relapse on the chalkboard or newsprint: (1) Hanging out with using friends; (2) skipping A.A. or N.A. meetings; (3) going to a bar "just for a game of pool." There are other more subtle signs that can also indicate whether someone is on the road of recovery or on the slide into relapse.

Pass out copies of the Relapse Warning Sign Worksheet and have the group complete it. Afterward, ask group members to share their personal relapse warning signs with the rest of the group. Specific examples are very helpful. Use questions like the following to discuss the signs:

■ Are you able to recognize when you are in a relapse-prone situation?
■ What do you do to handle these situations?
■ Have you relapsed before? What lead up to that relapse?
■ Can you depend on will power alone to keep yourself from relapsing?

Go on to ask group members to identify things they can do when they are experiencing relapse warning signs. You may want to ask group members to think of something they could do for each of the five relapse warning signs they circled on their worksheet (since these five are the signs that are most personally indicative of relapse) and to write what they would do about this on the bottom of the worksheet.

Relapse Warning Signs Worksheet

Check any relapse warning signs that apply to you.

___ Overly confident

___ Setting unrealistic goals

___ Sure you'll never drink again

___ Forgetting to be grateful

___ Constant boredom

___ Minimizing problems

___ Complacency

___ Covering up feelings

___ Secret dissatisfaction

___ Can't handle stress

___ Dishonesty

___ Defensiveness

___ Avoiding problems

___ Pulling away from sponsor

___ Loneliness

___ Depression

___ Rejecting advice

___ Blaming others

___ Difficulty sleeping

___ Reduced work or school effort

___ Talk of "good old days"

___ Sporadic meeting attendance

___ Visiting bars

___ More time with drinking friends

___ Preoccupation with drinking

___ Forgetting to take antabuse

___ Thinking "one last time"

___ Less time with program friends

Additional relapse warning signs for you:

_____   _____

_____   _____

_____   _____

From the group of warning signs you checked, circle the five which would most likely show up in your life if you began moving towards relapse.

Helping Hand

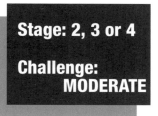

Stage: 2, 3 or 4

Challenge:
MODERATE

OBJECTIVES: ▶ To prevent relapse episodes
To broaden and strengthen support networks

MATERIALS: ▶ Copies of the **Helping Hand Contract Worksheet**

DESCRIPTION: ▶ Group members complete a contract, involving family and friends, who will encourage a positive change in behavior should group members come close to a relapse episode.

PROCEDURE: ▶ Tell group members that since people abstaining from alcohol or other drugs often do not notice their own relapse warning signs, it can be helpful to ask for help from family, A.A. or N.A. members, sponsors, a counselor, or other friends. The Helping Hand Contract Worksheet will help encourage these people to share their concerns.

Distribute copies of the worksheet. Go through it with group members and have them fill it out. Explain that having others sign the contract is like building a safety net of helping hands to support them lest they fall back into using alcohol or other drugs. Direct group members to ask people who know them well, have regular contact with them, and are aware of their commitment to sobriety to read and sign the contract. Tell members to bring their signed contracts back to a future group session where you will make copies of them to be given to those who signed.

Helping Hand Contract Worksheet

It's possible for me to be headed down the road towards a relapse without my realizing it. I value your opinion, and I need you to tell me when you have any concerns about my sobriety. Here is my list of warning signs indicating I might be heading back into alcohol or other drug use:

1. _____
2. _____
3. _____
4. _____
5. _____

If you notice any of these signs or see me getting into trouble in other ways, please tell me. Don't wait until it's too late. If you do point out a concern to me, I promise I will try to listen without becoming defensive because I know you care about me. If I don't listen to your concerns, or if my behavior doesn't improve, I want you to take these steps: (Contact my sponsor or counselor, insist I return to a treatment program, kick me out of the house.)

1. _____
2. _____
3. _____

For family and friends to sign:

If I notice the above relapse warning signs, I will speak up and let you know of my concerns.

Signed: _____ _____

                     _____ _____

                     _____ _____

For you to sign:

I promise to listen to any concerns you might have about my sobriety and to follow through with any recommendations made by my counselor.

_____

The Grieving Process

OBJECTIVES: ▶ To learn the stages of the grieving process
To prepare for possible grief reactions when quitting the abuse of alcohol and other drugs

MATERIALS: ▶ None required

DESCRIPTION: ▶ Group members learn about the stages of grieving and discuss their possible grief reactions to abstaining from alcohol and other drugs.

PROCEDURE: ▶ Begin this session by drawing from the For Your Information section to make a presentation that conveys to the group the five stages of the grieving process. Afterward, to make certain everyone understands the grief process, ask the group to think of a hypothetical loss (e.g., the death of a loved one) and then to describe possible grief reactions.

After discussing the hypothetical situation, have group members imagine themselves quitting their use of all alcohol and other drugs and to imagine their personal grief reactions. For example: Ken might see himself becoming very angry (anger stage) that he can't use any longer, especially when he sees his buddies going off to a party; Nancy thinks she would fight the fact that she even needs to quit, and instead would want to cut down on how often she drinks (bargaining stage).

Give group members a few minutes to contemplate this, then use the remaining time to allow them to share their grief reactions.

For Your Information

The Grieving Process

Grief is a reaction to any heart-felt loss. Probably the first example that comes to mind is the death of a loved one, but there are many other examples, such as moving away, quitting the service, ending a relationship.

Adults who abuse alcohol and other drugs do so for a myriad of reasons, but it's safe to say that alcohol and other drugs do something for them, be it making them feel popular, attractive, happy, or whatever. Because alcohol and other drugs do this, chemically dependent people develop a love affair with alcohol and other drugs. When they quit this love affair, they will not only grieve the loss of the alcohol or other drug, but also the loss of an identity, a group of friends, rituals, excitement, pleasure. Of course, they don't really lose all these things, but it certainly feels like it. It's important for people struggling to quit using alcohol and other drugs to understand that it's normal for them to grieve the loss of their drug-centered life-style.

Grieving has five stages, first identified by Elizabeth Kübler-Ross in her work with dying patients. Listed below are these stages and the thoughts typical of someone who has been diagnosed terminally ill with cancer:

Denial	"No, it can't be true. I've just got the flu."
Anger	"These quack doctors don't know anything."
Bargaining	"I'll take my pills, but I'm never going to go through chemotherapy."
Depression	"What's the use in trying."
Acceptance	"I've got cancer but I'm going to enjoy every day I've got left."

An adult who quits smoking pot and who is grieving it might have this to say:

Denial	"I don't have a problem."
Anger	"Hey, get off my back. You're my problem!"
Bargaining	"I'll quit hanging around with Bill, but I'm still going to go to parties."
Depression	"I'm going to be the only non-drinking person in my unit."
Acceptance	"As long as I stay clean and sober, I'm finally going to make something of my life!"

These stages are experienced in sequence, but it's common to return to a stage previously experienced. A person might vacillate between denial, anger, and bargaining for a long time before moving into the last two stages. She or he might even return briefly to the first three stages. Grieving group members will work through these stages differently and at their own pace.

Futuring Activities

Alcoholics Anonymous members live by a famous slogan, "One day at a time."
At first blush, this adage may seem to counsel us not to worry about or plan for
the future. Nothing could be further from the truth. A.A. members realize that
when it comes to the future, our task is not to foresee it, but to empower it.

Futuring activities are designed to help group members learn the skills that will
allow them to evaluate their experiences, anticipate problems, set appropriate
goals, and make plans to achieve those goals. The purpose of these activities,
then, is not to foretell group members' future, but to give them one.

Setting Goals

OBJECTIVES: ▶ To encourage goal setting
To learn problem-solving skills

MATERIALS: ▶ Copies of the **Setting Goals Worksheet**

DESCRIPTION: ▶ Group members complete a worksheet that helps them clarify and work towards a personal goal.

PROCEDURE: ▶ Begin this session by asking group members to choose and share a personal problem they are experiencing (e.g., fighting with a spouse or trying to quit drinking) that they would like to solve. After everyone has shared a problem with the rest of the group, distribute copies of the Setting Goals Worksheet and ask the group to complete it. You may wish to go over the worksheet to make sure group members understand it.

After everyone has finished, ask them to share their work with the group. Don't hesitate to offer suggestions if a group member chooses a goal that seems too difficult to obtain or outlines what he or she won't do rather than what he or she will do.

Ask group members to keep their worksheets so they can refer to them while working toward their goals. Record these personal goals for your own reference so that you can evaluate their progress as they work toward their stated goals. During the next session of group, members can discuss their progress towards reaching their goals.

NOTES: ▶ Instead of a one-week review, you may wish to wait several weeks, or follow up on group members' progress with a brief discussion several times during the course of the group.

Setting Goals Worksheet

1. A problem I have:

2. What I want to change about this problem (goal):

3. What I can do to help make this change happen:

   1.

   2.

   3.

4. What I am willing to do to help bring about this change:

   1.

   2.

   3.

5. I am willing to do this by this date:

Goals and Decisions

Stage: 1,2 or 3

Challenge:
MODERATE

OBJECTIVES: ▶ To reinforce personal decisions
To identify personal needs and issues
To encourage goal setting

MATERIALS: ▶ Writing paper

DESCRIPTION: ▶ Group members identify and set personal goals for themselves and then share them with the rest of the group.

PROCEDURE: ▶ Ask group members to think about any personal issues or problems they have identified as a result of participating in their group. Pass out sheets of paper and ask them to write these personal issues in the form of a goal they can work toward. Typical examples include quitting drinking, talking more often about feelings, or learning more about how problems with chemical dependence have affected them.

Also ask the group to record any personal decisions they've made for themselves, such as not hanging around a particular person any longer, not drinking anymore, or attending Narcotics Anonymous.

After group members have written their goals and decisions, ask them to share their answers with the group. Encourage the rest of the group to give feedback after a group member has finished sharing goals and decisions. For example, the group might remind a group member about a time she had told the group she really needs to go running rather than heading towards the fridge for a beer when she gets angry at her husband. The group member can then add this to her list.

NOTES: ▶ This activity can be used either in the early stages of group or later on, after group members have developed some awareness as to how their alcohol or other drug use affects their lives. Using this activity during the initial sessions of group helps group members clarify goals which, in turn, gives a sense of direction for the group. However, if you feel that group members won't be able to identify personal issues or goals at the early stage of group, save this activity until their awareness has been raised. Or use this activity twice and compare the goals. Group members might find their personal goals to be quite different the second time around.

Who I Want to Be

OBJECTIVES:

To encourage personal goal setting

MATERIALS:

Copies of the **Who I Want to Be Worksheet**

DESCRIPTION:

Group members describe what kind of people they want to be ten years from now (happy, confident, mature, sensitive) and discuss what steps need to be taken to ensure this will happen.

PROCEDURE:

Point out to the group that when we discuss the future, we often think in terms of where we want to live or what we want to be doing—"What do you want to be or do?" Go on to explain that when it comes to the future, it's also important to consider *who* we want to be. For example, do we want to be someone that others turn to for help? Someone that little children like? Do we want to be quiet and thoughtful or the life of the party? Years from now do we want to still be in trouble with alcohol and other drugs, or do we want this problem to be behind us?

Distribute copies of the Who I Want to Be Worksheet and have group members fill it out on their own. When everyone is finished, ask group members to share what they wrote with the group. After they have shared both the "Now" and "Future" categories, ask group members to describe what is different between the first and second category. Once a group member has identified what needs changing (for example, "I want to be more outgoing in the future"), ask what needs to happen for this change to take place. If the individual is unable to think of a plan, ask the group for suggestions. For example, a group member might, in the future, like to be the kind of person who has his "act together," whereas now he is always in some kind of trouble. The group might suggest to him that every day he spend a few minutes talking with a good friend about how he's feeling and what he's planning on doing before he makes impulsive decisions.

NOTES:

If group members don't offer one another feedback, and look to you for advice, resist giving it. Instead, ask a group member what he or she thinks this group member should do to make his or her desired changes.

Who I Want to Be Worksheet

Now

Below, list eight examples that describe the kind of person you are now—not what you do, but who you are and what you are like. Examples could include "I'm outgoing," "I worry about things too much," "I'm a party animal," or "I'm a good listener."

1. _____
2. _____
3. _____
4. _____
5. _____
6. _____
7. _____
8. _____

Future

Now think about the kind of person you'd like to be ten years from now. Do you want to reduce your shyness and be more outgoing? Do you want to no longer worry so much about what other people think about you? Go ahead and dream. List eight qualities you would like to have as a part of you ten years from now:

1. _____
2. _____
3. _____
4. _____
5. _____
6. _____
7. _____
8. _____

Stumbling Blocks

OBJECTIVES: ▶ To identify obstacles to making positive changes
To discover ways to cope with obstacles to positive change

MATERIALS: ▶ Copies of the **Stumbling Blocks Worksheet**

DESCRIPTION: ▶ Group members identify and discuss those things in their lives that prevent them from making positive changes.

PROCEDURE: ▶ Begin this session by asking group members to define what is meant by "taking care of yourself." If need be, steer them in the direction of defining this concept as: all those things we do that are healthy, positive, and affirming. This includes everything from getting up for work to following through on promises, from talking about feelings to confronting someone when we are upset with that person's behavior, from quitting getting high to dealing with stress constructively. List the group's ideas on the chalkboard or newsprint.

Point out to the group that none of us are always successful in taking care of ourselves. Explain that today's activity can, however, help us understand what interferes with our ability to be good to ourselves.

Distribute copies of the Stumbling Blocks Worksheet and allow group members to complete it on their own. Afterward, spend the remaining time discussing their answers. Use questions like the following to foster discussion:

■ How many of you have similar stumbling blocks?
■ What are these common stumbling blocks?
■ Have you always had stumbling blocks in your life? Why or why not?
■ Have you tried to get rid of these stumbling blocks before?

Stumbling Blocks Worksheet

For each block below fill in something that interferes with your being able to take care of yourself. Examples of such stumbling blocks might include: a certain friend, cocaine, not getting enough sleep, alcohol, a girlfriend, or television.

Below, write how you can deal with these stumbling blocks or at least avoid them.

1. _____

2 _____

3. _____

4 _____

5. _____

6 _____

7. _____

8 _____

Material for this worksheet is adapted from Johnson Institute's *From Peer Pressure to Peer Support* by Shelley MacKay Freeman (see Resources section).

What I Need to Change

OBJECTIVES: ▶ To identify what we must change to successfully quit using alcohol and other drugs
To encourage constructive peer influence

MATERIALS: ▶ Writing paper

DESCRIPTION: ▶ The support group as a whole outlines for each group member the conditions that should be changed in order for that particular group member to be able to quit using alcohol and other drugs.

PROCEDURE: ▶ Begin this session by asking group members to list on the blackboard or newsprint the things that would get in the way for someone who was trying to quit drinking and using other drugs, for example, hanging around with friends who get drunk frequently, going to a party where lots of drugs would be available, frequenting bars, avoiding talking about what was going on inside, or being stressed out all the time.

Once group members have made an extensive list, ask for a volunteer to be the focus of attention. Assuming the group is familiar with this person's background, ask the rest of the group to identify what this person must change in order to quit using alcohol and other drugs.

Ask one group member to be the recorder and to write down all suggestions on a piece of paper to give to the group member who is being given feedback. Often the group will be hesitant to speak out. In such a case, go around the group circle and request that each person name one thing that should be changed. If the volunteer becomes defensive, trying to debate the suggestions offered, explain that he or she will have a chance to speak after everyone has finished making suggestions. Be sure to share your suggestions also.

When the group has finished offering suggestions, and the volunteer has had a chance to respond, ask him or her to choose someone for the group to focus on next.

NOTES: This activity requires that group members be familiar with each other's background and personal lives in order to be successful.

From Now On

OBJECTIVES: ▶ To encourage goal setting
To support personal changes

MATERIALS: ▶ Copies of the **From Now On Worksheet**

DESCRIPTION: ▶ Group members review what they've learned about themselves during the course of group and identify new behaviors they'll continue to practice.

PROCEDURE: ▶ Review previous sessions with the group, pointing out various concepts and skills learned. For example the importance of naming and expressing feelings appropriately, developing refusal skills, recognizing how alcohol and other drugs have caused problems. After the review, ask group members to reflect quietly on the personal lessons they've learned during group. Meanwhile, hand out copies of the From Now On Worksheet and give group members time to complete it.

Once group members have finished, ask each to share with the group what he or she wrote. If, after some shares, you believe he or she has forgotten an important personal lesson, call it to this person's attention and encourage him or her to add it to the worksheet.

From Now On Worksheet

Based on what you have learned in group, list the things you will do differently from now on.

Instead
of _____

From now on,
I'm going to _____

Instead
of _____

From now on,
I'm going to _____

Instead
of _____

From now on,
I'm going to _____

Instead
of _____

From now on,
I'm going to _____

Instead
of _____

From now on,
I'm going to _____

Group Evaluations

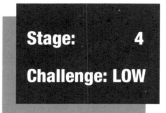

Stage: 4

Challenge: LOW

OBJECTIVES:

To solicit feedback and collect data about the group experience
To improve the effectiveness of future groups

MATERIALS:

Copies of the **Evaluation Worksheet**

DESCRIPTION:

Group members evaluate their group experience.

PROCEDURE:

Hand out copies of the Evaluation Worksheets. Tell group members not to write their names on the worksheets, but to complete them anonymously. Encourage them to answer the questions honestly. Let them know that their feedback will be used to make the group experience better next time around for new group members.

NOTES:

Although this activity is best employed during a final group session, it's a good idea to do so at the beginning of such a session. Remember, a final group session is usually an emotional time for the group members, and they may resist having to complete paperwork when more emotional issues are on their minds: saying good-bye, dealing with unfinished business, wondering what they will do now that the group experience is over.

Group Evaluation Worksheet

To All Group Members:
Would you please take a minute to fill out this evaluation of group?
Do not put your name on this. Thank you.

1. **Was your group a valuable experience for you?**
    No   Somewhat   Yes
    1   2   3   4   5   6   7   8   9   10

2. **How would you rate your group leader's ability to lead the group?**
    Poor   Fair   Good
    1   2   3   4   5   6   7   8   9   10

3. **How helpful was your group leader for you personally?**
    Of little help   Very helpful
    1   2   3   4   5   6   7   8   9   10

4. **List three things that you learned in group.**

    1.

    2.

    3.

5. **How did this group most help you?**

6. **What didn't you like about this group?**

7. **How could this group be improved?**

The Last Word

OBJECTIVES: ▶ To encourage closure to the group experience

MATERIALS: ▶ None required

DESCRIPTION: ▶ Group members say their "good-byes" to the group and one another.

PROCEDURE: ▶ Begin a discussion by asking group members to reflect on all previous group sessions, especially those events that were humorous, emotionally intense, anxiety producing, etc. Record these events on the chalkboard or newsprint in a chronological order by constructing a time line covering all sessions of the group. All of this will help members realize all the work they have done while participating in the group.

After this discussion, ask group members to hold hands in a circle. Invite all group members to share their feelings and "good-bye" statements with the rest of the group. Use the following sentence stems to help them put their feelings into statements:

■ Now that our group is over I'm really going to miss...
■ One thing I really appreciate about all of you is...
■ I would like you all to know that I...
■ I will never forget...

Resources

NOTE: ▶ The following materials are available from the Johnson Institute, and can be ordered by writing or calling the Johnson Institute at 7205 Ohms Lane, Minneapolis, Minnesota 55439-5165, 1-800-231-5165 or 612-831-1630. An order form is available for your use on page 115. A free catalog is available upon request.

BOOKS: ▶ *Alcohol Is A Drug, Too,* David Wilmes. ISBN 1-56246-057-9

Choices and Consequences, Dick Shaefer. ISBN 0-935908-42-0

Commitment to Sobriety: A Relapse Prevention Guide for Adults in Recovery, Martin Fleming. ISBN 56246-023-4

Conducting Support Groups for Students Affected by Chemical Dependence, Martin Fleming. ISBN 0-935908-51-X

Diagnosing and Treating Co-Dependence: A Guide for Professionals Who Work with Chemical Dependents, Their Spouses, and Children, Timmen Cermak, M.D. ISBN 0-935908-32-3

Evaluating and Treating Adult Children of Alcoholics: Volume One: Evaluation, Timmen Cermak, M.D. ISBN 0-935908-64-1

Evaluating and Treating Adult Children of Alcoholics: Volume Two: Treatment, Timmen Cermak, M.D. ISBN 0-935908-66-8

Everything You Need to Know About Chemical Dependence: Vernon Johnson's Complete Guide for Families. ISBN 0-935908-53-6

I'll Quit Tomorrow, Vernon Johnson, D.D. ISBN 0-06-250433-9

Intervention: How to Help Someone Who Doesn't Want Help, Vernon Johnson, D.D. ISBN 0-935908-31-5

Making Choices: How to Prevent Alcohol and Other Drug Problems at Work. ISBN 1-56246-097-8

101 Support Group Activities for Teenagers Affected by Someone Else's Alcohol/Drug Use, Martin Fleming. ISBN 1-565246-038-2

101 Support Group Activities for Teenagers At Risk for Chemical Dependence or Related Problems, Martin Fleming. ISBN 1-56246-042-0

101 Support Group Activities for Teenagers Recovering from Chemical Dependence, Martin Fleming. ISBN 1-56246-041-2

Anger: How to Handle It During Recovery. ISBN 1-56246-009-9

Alcoholism: A Treatable Disease. ISBN 0-935908-37-4

Chemical Dependence and Recovery: A Family Affair. ISBN 0-935908-00-5

Chemical Dependence: Yes, You Can Do Something. ISBN 0-935908-3508

Resources

National Organizations

The following groups and organizations can provide additional information on preventing alcohol and other drug use.

Al-Anon Family Group Headquarters
1372 Broadway
New York, NY 10018-0862
(212) 302-7240

Alateen
1372 Broadway
New York, NY 10018-0862
(212) 302-7240

Alcoholics Anonymous (AA)
General Service Office
P.O. Box 459
Grand Central Station
New York, NY 10163
(212) 686-1100

Children of Alcoholics Foundation, Inc. (COAF)
555 Madison Avenue, Fourth Floor
New York, NY 10022
(212) 754-0656

Families Anonymous
World Service Office
P.O. Box 528
Van Nuys, CA 91408
(818) 989-7841

Institute on Black Chemical Abuse (IBCA)
2616 Nicollet Avenue South
Minneapolis, MN 55408
(612) 871-7878

Johnson Institute
7205 Ohms Lane
Minneapolis, MN 55439-2159
(800) 231-5165

Narcotics Anonymous (NA)
World Services Offices
P.O. Box 9999
Van Nuys, CA 91409
(818) 780-3951

National Clearinghouse for Alcohol and Drug Information (NCADI)
11426 Rockville Pike
Rockville, MD 20852
(301) 468-2600

ORDER FORM

BILL TO:	SHIP TO: (if different from BILL TO:)

Name _____   Name _____

Address _____   Address _____

_____   _____

City _____ State _____ Zip _____   City _____ State _____ Zip _____

ATTENTION: _____   **ATTENTION:** _____

Daytime Phone: (   ) _____   Daytime Phone: (   ) _____

PURCHASE ORDER NO. _____   TAX EXEMPT NO. _____

❑ Individual Order   ❑ Group or Organization Order

If Ordering for a Group or Organization:

Group Name _____

Please send me a free copy(ies) of Johnson Institute's:	❑ ___ Publications and Films Catalog(s) ❑ ___ Training Calendar(s) ❑ *Observer*, a quarterly newsletter

PLEASE SEND ME:

QTY.	ORDER NO.	TITLE	PRICE EACH	TOTAL COST

For film/video titles, please specify: ❑ 1/2" VHS   ❑ 3/4" U-Matic   ❑ 1/2" Beta   ❑ 16mm

---

SHIPPING AND HANDLING

Order Amount	U.S.	Outside U.S.
$0–25.00	$5.50	$6.50
$25.01–60.00	$7.00	$8.50
$60.01–130.00	$9.00	$11.25
$130.01–200.00	$11.25	$17.00
$200.01–300.00	$14.00	$21.00
$300.01–over	7%	12%

Please add $7.00 ($8.00 Canada) for any videotapes ordered

OFFICE USE ONLY

Order No. _____

Customer No. _____

❑ Payment enclosed
❑ Bill me
❑ Bill my credit card:

❑ MasterCard
❑ VISA
❑ American Express
❑ Discover

Expiration Date: _____

Signature on card: _____

Total Order _____
(Orders under $75.00 must be prepaid)

6.5% Sales Tax _____
(Minnesota Residents Only)

Shipping and Handling _____
(See Chart)

TOTAL _____

Have you ordered from the Johnson Institute before? **Yes** ❑   **No** ❑

If yes, how?   **Mail** ❑   **Phone** ❑

QVS, Inc.

JOHNSON INSTITUTE®

7205 Ohms Lane ❖ Minneapolis, Minnesota 55439-2159
(612) 831-1630 or toll-free: 1-800-231-5165

When the Johnson Institute first opened its doors in 1966, few people knew or believed that alcoholism was a disease. Fewer still thought that anything could be done to help the chemically dependent person other than to wait for him or her to "hit bottom" and then pick up the pieces.

We've spent over twenty years spreading the good news that chemical dependence is a treatable disease. Through our publications, films, video and audiocassettes, and our training and consultation services, we've given hope and help to hundreds of thousands of people across the country and around the world. The intervention and treatment methods we've pioneered have restored shattered careers, healed relationships with co-workers and friends, saved lives, and brought whole families back together.

Today the Johnson Institute is an internationally recognized leader in the field of chemical dependence intervention, treatment, and recovery. Individuals, organizations, and businesses, large and small, rely on us to provide them with the tools they need. Schools, universities, hospitals, treatment centers, and other health care agencies look to us for experience, expertise, innovation, and results. With care, compassion, and commitment, we will continue to reach out to chemically dependent persons, their families, and the professionals who serve them.

JOHNSON INSTITUTE®